AF431367

# CHANGE YOUR PERSPECTIVE CHANGE YOUR LIFE!

HOW WOULD YOU REFRAME YOUR MENTAL ATTITUDE TOWARDS EVERYDAY SITUATIONS TO FIND A POSITIVE PERSPECTIVE IN YOUR LIFE?

DR. AMIT DAS

Copyright © Dr. Amit Das
All Rights Reserved.

This book has been self-published with all reasonable efforts taken to make the material error-free by the author. No part of this book shall be used, reproduced in any manner whatsoever without written permission from the author, except in the case of brief quotations embodied in critical articles and reviews.

The Author of this book is solely responsible and liable for its content including but not limited to the views, representations, descriptions, statements, information, opinions and references ["Content"]. The Content of this book shall not constitute or be construed or deemed to reflect the opinion or expression of the Publisher or Editor. Neither the Publisher nor Editor endorse or approve the Content of this book or guarantee the reliability, accuracy or completeness of the Content published herein and do not make any representations or warranties of any kind, express or implied, including but not limited to the implied warranties of merchantability, fitness for a particular purpose. The Publisher and Editor shall not be liable whatsoever for any errors, omissions, whether such errors or omissions result from negligence, accident, or any other cause or claims for loss or damages of any kind, including without limitation, indirect or consequential loss or damage arising out of use, inability to use, or about the reliability, accuracy or sufficiency of the information contained in this book.

Made with ♥ on the Notion Press Platform
www.notionpress.com

To

All my bosses and mentors who made a difference in my professional career.

"You will benefit from winning the mental battle if you first learn how your brain works and then reprogram it. Determine the lies that your adversary wants you to believe. Recognise your mental triggers for negative thinking and stop using them. It doesn't matter what other people think of you. More significant is how people perceive you. You need to be ambitious, eager, aspirational, and possess the will and wish power to achieve everything. The only things that may lead you to the pinnacle of success in your life are your thoughts, ideas, words, and deeds. It's time to alter your perspective so that almighty can alter your life. You'll soon be able to live the life you've always wanted."

– Dr. Amit Das, Motivational Speaker, Leadership Coach , Counsellor, and Mentor.

# Contents

# Foreword

**Dear Reader,**

Thank you for taking the time to learn more about "Change Your Perspective Change Your Life!" and the rewarding outcome of increasing your personal productivity. This is a book with a stunning design that is packed with motivational sayings and tried-and-true advice on utilising optimism to build a life you love.

- How can you actually learn to love yourself?
- How to change unfavourable feelings into favourable ones?
- Is it possible to have permanent joy?

Life coaching expert Dr. Amit Das provides comprehensive solutions to all of these queries in this book. He survived hardship to become a source of inspiration for countless young people, and he now draws on his own experience and intuitive knowledge to motivate you. The only way you think that will define how best you have created your legacy in this life, regardless of where you are from, how educated you are, or the situations you find yourself in.

You'll realise that all really successful individuals could make it in their lives and leave their footprints after reading this book. This book provides the "magic bullet" you need, whether you want to make better-informed decisions in your life, land a new job, or just be happy. The majority of individuals wish they could be more beautiful, persuasive, and innovative. For years, gurus and "life coaches" have advised individuals to change the way they think and act in order to better their lives. However, a scientific study has shown that many of these tactics, such as group brainstorming and visualisation, are unsuccessful. Fortunately, you have access to quick-acting, myth-busting scientific solutions to a wide range of common issues in this book. Personal and professional success might be reached in less than an hour in many personal areas .

Dr. Amit Das, a motivational speaker, mentor, counsellor, and coach, will demonstrate how to take charge and unlock your latent potential via effective methods, regardless of your viewpoint being negative, positive, or somewhere in between.

This book is an enlightening voyage through one's own life, including your past, present, and future. You will re-vision and re-cast your life's tale as explorers in your own lives by discovering your deepest inspiration, your happiest emotions, and expressing your ambitions. The author tells readers how to gracefully navigate the difficulties of life while remaining energised and thoroughly grounded.

This book, which is extremely encouraging and inspirational, wants its readers to realise that a sunrise and a beautiful day always follow a long and gloomy night. Despite repeated failures, the author exhorts his readers to never give up since there is always a way out of any challenging circumstance. He discusses a variety of stressful scenarios that people encounter on a regular basis. Such as long-term illness, losing a loved one, being unemployed, and other frightful circumstances that might obstruct a person's path to achievement. The author provides his readers with a variety of guidelines to help them deal with all of these challenges.

The author will demonstrate to you how you may start to influence the world by altering the way you feel, think, speak, and act. Instead of merely existing, begin to grow! He covers many aspects including the human condition, discovering one's purpose in life, and the secret to long-lasting happiness. He takes us on a memorable trip with his priceless insights on these aspects of life, whether you're wanting to improve your relationships, realise your full potential, learn how to succeed at business, or even how you may give back to the world. He is one of the most well-known and in-demand mentor and life coach in India, having taught thousands of people. This book,"Change Your Perspective Change Your Life!," his passionate creation, distils his life experiences and teachings into a humorous, thought-provoking book that will assist you in aligning yourself with the life you desire.

This book will provide you with detailed instructions on how to discover the meaning and purpose of your life in order to feel fulfilled and like you're on the right track. Your life will essentially become more useful to you, the people around you, and eventually the world, if you have a feeling of purpose and meaning in it.

Dr. Amit Das gave a step-by-step guide for identifying and fulfilling your life's mission. It is jam-packed with important basic ideas that anybody can use to improve their quality of life, presented in engrossing bits of knowledge. Additionally, the author has a system of internal assistance to guarantee your success. This book, "Change Your Perspective Change Your Life," in an hour exhorts you to regain control over how you choose to spend your time, which will ultimately affect how your life turns out.

This book will assist you in understanding such concerns and reprogramming your daily life to produce more uplifting results. Dr. Amit Das sought out these solutions and invested many hours in his quest to improve himself; this book is a condensed version of such transformative encounters and ideas. You'll be helped by this book. In these uncertain times, do you wish someone could just tell you what to do and how to live your life? So the hunt is over right here. This book provides readers with useful "guidelines" that they may immediately put into practise in their daily lives.

The goal of this book is to encourage each reader to create their own legacy. Most people have the desire to pursue immortality. It inspires many people to start families, publish novels, compose music, create inventions, amass cash, or succeed in a myriad of professions. Even within your own family, immortality, or merely being remembered by future generations, is difficult to attain. Many of us experience this inner conflict of feeling aimless and unimportant.

The author of this book tells us a surprising truth about what motivates us. He lists purpose, along with esteem and contentment, as the three main components of human motivation. According to the author, this type of motivation is superior to conventional theories of motivation, which focus on rewards and the threat of punishment. You'll specifically gain more confidence around others thanks to the advice in this book.

You'll discover how to eliminate the imposter syndrome, stop people-pleasing, reduce self-doubt, understand where it actually comes from, how to read people more effectively, overcome the need for acceptance, stop people-pleasing, and much more.

Most people have the desire to pursue immortality. It inspires many people to start families, publish novels, compose music, create inventions, amass cash, or succeed in a myriad of professions. Even within your own family, immortality, or merely being remembered by future generations, is difficult to attain. Few people have ever met all four grandparents or even know anything about them. Generations pass away in a swirl of nothingness. That much is true. However, if you read this book and take bold action to become immortal, you may do so within your family, community, and, for a select few, globally. Everything is subject to your wishes. You may become eternal by reading this little book. And if you want assistance, get in touch with the author of this book.

Most of us are much more afraid of being alive and not knowing, so probably not. Overcome your fear and go with the flow of the universe; discover your higher purpose and become a role model for others. Live each day to the utmost and treat it as though it were your last. It is therefore evident that the book does not support any means of achieving physical immortality rather, it supports immortality in the truest sense—being remembered by countless generations. You can achieve immortality. This book, "Change Your Perspective Change Your Life!," which was inspired by personal experience, was born out of the author's long search for a step-by-step process to achieve perfect clarity and purpose in his own life.

By guiding you how to strive, understand, create, condition, envision, and savour, this book demonstrates how to find your life's purpose and then begin living it. The book is written in straightforward terms for the average reader; it is not a place for jargon or mysticism. It gives you options so you can go your own way, believe in your progress, and be confident enough to move forward.and after that. Your own dreams are the key; all you need is this book.

The author of the book provides you with techniques to train your mindset so that you can protect against negative ideas and cultivate the habit of positive thinking. It will show you how to develop positive thinking that will enable you to realise your full potential. You will achieve beyond your wildest expectations thanks to it.

This book offers you a tried-and-true method for developing a thorough grasp of who you are, a clear understanding of the purpose and direction you desire for your life, and how to develop into the kind of person you need to be in order to live that way. He outlines the guiding principles of intentional living that will enable you to take charge of your life rather than let it dominate you.

There is a fix for each issue. The chance of resolving the issue also arises when you discuss it someplace. He offers simple procedures that may be used to assess the feasibility of novel concepts. In this book, he has also included guidelines and strategies to prevent burnout. The wonderful part about all the concepts discussed in "Change Your Perspective Change Your Life" is that they are written and presented in such a way that they can be applied to nearly any circumstance.

Even better, you'll have a personal insight into how you really compare and what needs to change in you in order to alter the trajectory of your personal life. This book is a collection of brief talks on your life's critical factors to accomplishing your pursuits and thriving in life. Through this book, you will learn from top achievers, established leaders, and individuals how they have excelled in their lives. With the appropriate balance of your thoughts, speech, and actions, you may strengthen the version of yourself that brings you joy and success. The author has used a distinctive literary technique to create and communicate a message about success that is sure to be memorable and life-changing. This book outlines the essential success criteria that are truly important if you want to experience exceptional success in life.

You can do this by using the motivational self-help book. Anyone who reads it will benefit personally and psychologically from it. Dr. Amit Das discusses actions you can take to create a fulfilling, flourishing life, including: spending an hour in silence to develop your creative vision; going above and beyond to help others; letting your strengths guide your work; reflecting on your mistakes; learning to manage your time effectively; and much more. The book "Change Your Perspective Change Your Life" strives to set you free from the bonds of your shackling ideas so that you may overcome your restraints and let your souls soar.

You can now choose. Clicking the order button now can either transform your life for the better or worse for the foreseeable future compared to doing nothing.

*Life has this peculiar way of giving you what you want if you just won't take anything less than the greatest.*

Once again, thank you for taking the time to learn more about how you would reframe your mental attitude towards everyday situations to find a positive perspective in your life? Thank you for taking the time to read this book.

So, happy reading and learning to all my readers.

**Carpe diem.**

**Dr. Amit Das**

**Leadership Coach , Counsellor, and Mentor.**

# Preface

*Life is a game, so play it; life is a challenge, so face it; and life is an opportunity, so seize it.*

What would it be like to be unconstrained and to fly above your limitations? What can you do every day to find tranquilly and inner peace? These issues are addressed in this book in a straightforward yet deep manner. This book will alter the way you interact with both yourself and the outside world, regardless of whether this is your first foray into inner space or you have dedicated your whole life to the inward trip. You'll learn what you can do to stop the repetitive thoughts and feelings that are limiting your consciousness.

*Your attitude is the first step on the path to a happy life, and you have influence over your perspective.*

I will demonstrate how the growth of awareness may help you all in the present and let go of upsetting memories and beliefs that prevent you from finding pleasure and self-realisation.

**"Success is not final, failure is not fatal: it is the courage to continue that counts"- Winston Churchill**

When individuals have a sense of purpose, productivity rises because this fosters job satisfaction and creates an internal drive for excellence that is considerably stronger than monetary rewards or the prospect of punishment. People who have a strong sense of purpose are also more equipped to adjust and recover in the face of a disaster. Any person who is motivated by their work's purpose is better able to stay motivated and actively engaged in it even in the face of adversity than those who are not.

- Have you ever questioned why some people appear to understand things more readily than others?
- Are you weary of holding out for your life to improve?
- How long are you prepared to wait for a miraculous transformation in your circumstances?

You will discover what it takes to build the life you want in this straightforward, quick-paced book. In this book, I will urge my readers to try some tried-and-true workouts, suggestions, and tactics that may transform their lives in unimaginable ways!

In fact, it's been estimated that a whopping 95% of people are unsure about their life goals. I was inspired when I realised how successful I had been. After seeing the incredible results for myself and realising how it could help others, I was inspired to compile everything into a single, concise book. You are living your life on purpose when you are enthusiastic about it. If you've ever had trouble figuring out your life's passion or purpose, you may have found that it's really challenging to find answers to these questions by merely pondering them. This book is organised using a special approach based on simple habit adjustments that make you face your fears, set practical objectives, and start succeeding in every aspect of your life. Don't settle; begin acting now to lead the life you choose. Anyone who is feeling a little lost, uncertain of what they want, or unsure of which way to go should read "Change Your Perspective

Change Your Life."

This book will distil my decades of research, practise, and instruction to:

- Describe paradigms and how they influence every decision you make.
- Instructions on creating your own paradigm shift.
- Show you how to swap out a paradigm that isn't working for you with a fresh one so you can start living the life you actually desire.

This book would assist you in addressing and finding solutions to all of life's most important concerns. What are you still holding out for? You can create and sustain it by using the resources you already have. Join me on this adventure to discover what true happiness is. You can create and sustain it by utilising the resources you already have. It's an expensive game that so many of us play to learn by making mistakes, often again. You can only truly achieve success in life by developing self-mastery, which you may do by using the create your legacy tree paradigm. Then, rather than taking years, your own growth will direct you toward the accomplishment of empowering objectives. Your legacy has four primary legs—love, health, freedom, and purpose—can be strengthened and balanced, guiding you toward positive decisions, worthwhile experiences, and satisfying connections. This is not just a book; rather, it presents the scientifically supported tactics mentioned inside in an interesting, easily comprehensible manner that will inform, amuse, and motivate you. You may have the foresight and self-assurance to build your own prosperous future. Let's start by claiming your very own happiness tree right away!

I wrote this collection of thoughts with folks who recognise the value of leaving a legacy in mind, but who are unsure of why they are alive or what they should be doing with their life in mind. It is a collection that will inspire both creatives in general and those who have never thought of themselves as creative or as capable of creating something admirable. These concepts should be read and digested as if they were a collection of flashcards. Examine each of these chapters , then choose one. Before attempting another, give it your complete attention. Each chapter comes with some thought-provoking points on its core.

It is a comprehensive approach that offers some realistic, scientific, easy-to-implement, but extremely powerful tactics to assist you in realising your actual potential and achieving the happiness and prosperity of your dreams! So train yourself to be in command of yourself and let the world see your unique brightness!

It's crucial for college students, recent grads, and anybody else who either hates their job or needs a change to become a more significant and real version of themselves. Are you already there? Do you understand the meaning of life? Have you figured out your passions and what you love to do? The two concepts that most define and affect the direction of your life are purpose and passion. You get enthused about life when you are passionate. Your purpose illuminates the way ahead and gives you confidence and courage.

*You can achieve anything you can dream of!*

In the free and easily accessible information era, there is no longer a necessity for individuals to overload their heads with knowledge. The war may be lost by those who regurgitate; those who innovate will plough their own path and triumph. Beacuase there is a clear distinction between winners and losers. Don't give up, because if you do, you've already lost. In the end, you have no right to complain to anybody about anything if you're not prepared to stand up for yourself. Hence, living in complaint is not worth it. Utilise it to the fullest. Your final day is unknown to you. Live your life to the fullest, in whatever way you see fit.

> *Losers give up at the drop of a hat, whereas winners spend time persevering through difficulties.*

Many people think that significant, life-affirming experiences are what characterise success, pleasure, and fulfilment. We may create the life we desire and a life that is worth living by maintaining consistency with key routines and behaviors. I would explain the actions you may follow to achieve your goals in terms of your life, relationships, and job. It all starts with how we begin each day. You'll be on the right track to figuring out exactly what you want from life and how you want to live it after you make some tiny changes to your morning routine. The book delves into the science behind why these processes work and the most effective methods to put them into practise on a daily basis, covering everything from preparing at night to incorporating little life hacks into your morning routine. You can improve your morning and increase your productivity, drive, and happiness.

Unfortunately, a lot of us spend our whole lives looking for our true calling and interests since they do not come to us naturally. Additionally, there are occasions when they are right in front of your eyes but you fail to see them.

Humans are pleasure-seeking creatures, but if you let pleasure dictate how your life unfolds, you'll never discover your passion and purpose. Do you ever feel as though you don't belong where you are? If that occurs to you, you might want to reconsider your decision. By reading this book, you may change the way you think, uncover your passion and purpose, and locate the place where you belong. Your desire to live can be killed by trying to fit in; you may never find a setting where your abilities and skills are valued and embraced. Also, it feels like life is a never-ending battle to please other people. In this book, I will help you to overcome some of your fears; strengthen your mental fortitude; discover your passion and purpose; feel better about yourself; and reframe your life goals.

*Life is a wonderful adventure that should be enjoyed to the fullest every day. The fact that life is a wonderful gift does not, however, imply that you always wake up ready to grasp the day.*

In order to inspire and direct readers to want, pursue, and fulfil their earthly purposes—or to strive to yield abundant fruit and be a benefit to almighty, mankind, and all of creation—this book discusses methodical ideas. It aims to instil a lifestyle of purpose in the reader so that, by almighty's grace , they may live by a plan, desire to be productive, and ultimately fulfil the almighty's purpose.

We were all made to provide solutions to the world's numerous problems and challenges and make it a more pleasant and safe place to live. All men must abandon selfish, avaricious, haphazard, fruitless, and evil lifestyles in order to live intentionally and make wise choices regarding our everyday activities in order to produce a lot of fruits. There are many abilities, spiritual gifts, and skills that may be used to improve the world and bring glory to almighty. Everyone has the ability to solve at least one specific problem for someone, and this should be realised. One is set to be directed, ideally, to discover his or her purpose or at least become highly fruitful by reading "Change Your Perspective Change Your Life." You can now choose by clicking the order button to either transform your life for the better or worse for the foreseeable future compared to doing nothing.

*What you do today, or what you did in the past, should not limit what you can accomplish moving forward.*

No matter how you currently define success, this short but mighty book called "Change Your Perspective Change Your Life" will undoubtedly change the way you think about and define it. This includes a wide range of remarkable stories and examples. The message will strike a chord with you deeply and leave you feeling deeply responsible for how you decide to accomplish the success you want. These include initiative, enthusiasm, optimism, decision-making, using failure to your advantage, selecting heroes carefully, managing oneself, managing one's boss, managing others, and leading others.

*Do you believe that you are not successful and that only others are?*

This book primarily discusses the fundamental mental skills required as a basis for the reader to construct a successful, happy, and fulfilling life. If you approach the book with this in mind, you may rapidly see how the recommendations presented can help you become the person you really want to be and get personally connected with them. This book will hold your hand as you embark on this incredible adventure of self-transformation and self-growth, and personality development is a trip worth taking. This book is with real-life quotes from business leaders from all walks of life who used the science of 30 minutes of successful planning to perfect their trade and rise to the top of their profession will inspire and amuse readers along the way. Even when life gets wilder, even crazier, learn how to develop fresh and correct plans in as little as 30 minutes.

Everyone aspires to have a more successful life, but sadly, very few people know how to take the necessary measures to get there. The good news is that, regardless of your exact objectives, if you use everything you're going to learn in this book, you will succeed in every aspect of your life.

You may live your life to its fullest and highest potential by following the advice in this book. A must-read book about new discoveries and life techniques, as well as how to be confident in public. It might be challenging to overcome the obstacles that life presents. Situations like severe health issues or shattered relationships are handled differently by various people. In order to give readers a wide range of options, Inspirational Stories compiles several new-age self-improvement techniques and complementary treatment modalities.

Success and achievement are not the same things, despite the fact that accomplishment is sometimes connected with success. When you try to achieve particular goals, you call it an accomplishment when you get the desired results. In essence, it refers to the outcomes you anticipate or plan for. Success is the result or benefit of a goal that has been attained. The meaning of achievement with each objective you complete, you move closer to financial security and a prosperous life. Through this book, you will learn from top achievers, established leaders, and individuals who have excelled in their fields. Every day, read just one definition and one chapter. Think about it, eat it up, and accept it. Own it. Allow the revelations to permeate your spirit and give you the insight, drive, and inspiration you need to release the genuinely exceptional performance that is inside you.

Welcome to success and happiness!

*The best thing we can do as we work to increase our effectiveness in a world that is getting more complicated and competitive is to constantly sharpen the saw. Reminding you that we are not supposed to be static but to constantly sharpen the saw is exactly what this book seeks to achieve.*

**- Dr. Amit Das, Motivational Speaker, Leadership Coach , Counsellor, and Mentor.**

# Acknowledgements

At the outset, I will thank my family for supporting me throughout the journey of writing my book and encouraging me to live my dreams; my son has always been instrumental in giving his inspiration to complete the writing of this book. Despite the fact that I am listed as the author of this book,**"Change Your Perspective Change Your Life!,"** would not have been published if I had depended entirely on my own talents. Creating this book required more than anything—it took a family of dedicated and caring people who were always prepared to lend a hand.

Writing a book while working full-time is no simple task, so I'd want to express my gratitude to my amazing coworkers who act as cheerleaders in equal measure. Thank you, too, to my students and clients for your patience and unflinching support while I worked on this book!

Thank you to everyone who has listened to me argue for doing everything you can to make your life, including your work life, more progressive. I appreciate everyone's assistance throughout the process. This book would not have been possible without each of you having had an impact on my life in some manner.

Lastly, I would like to thank all the people with whom I have been associated. You gave me power. I would like to thank Notion Press for publishing my book. Finally, thank you all for gifting your time to read this book.

I'd want to convey my heartfelt appreciation to the almighty God for bestowing his blessings and being so gracious.

# CHAPTER ONE

# Changing Perspective And Gaining Happiness In Life

*"Success is not the key to happiness. Happiness is the key to success. If you love what you are doing, you will be successful."-Herman Cain*

*People who are happy plan their acts but not their outcomes.*

The goal of human life is to escape the suffering of a material existence and find happiness. Happiness is something we strive for all the time, yet we frequently fall short. Happiness may appear for a moment, but it is fleeting. We cannot avoid suffering, even when we may not desire it. We need to comprehend what is causing our difficulties in the first place so we can fix them. Since the beginning of time, we have been stuck in this material world, and the enjoyment we seek here is fleeting and deceptive.

*Happiness is the art of never holding in your mind the memory of any unpleasant thing that has passed.*

We participate in a variety of pious and immoral acts that keep us increasingly tied to this material world in search of such bliss. When we adhere to these three principles, all of the material contamination and sins are washed away, and as a result, we are reinstated in our true constitutional position of limitless pleasure and contentment. Our sorrows are caused by our sinful reactions.

**"The moments of happiness we enjoy take us by surprise. It is not that we seize them, but that they seize us."-Ashley Montagu**

We cannot avoid suffering, even when we may not desire it. The Vedanta-stra states that we are spiritual beings, an integral part of the Supreme Lord Sri Krishna, and that we are naturally joyful creatures, or nandamayo 'bhyst. So why do we endure pain? How can we find our lost happiness again and live happy lives? Let's first identify the underlying causes of the issues that are ruining our lives. Since the beginning of time, we have been trapped in this material world, and the enjoyment we seek here is fleeting and deceptive.

*Every day, remind yourself that you can choose to be happy. Nobody, nothing, or success can make you happy; nobody else can either.*

We participate in a variety of pious and immoral acts that keep us increasingly tied to this material world in the pursuit of such happiness. When we adhere to life principles, all of the material contamination and sins are washed away, and as a result, we are reinstated in our true constitutional position of limitless bliss and contentment.

This is a wonderful illustration of how you might occasionally truly "find" your purpose? When you are exhausted, it is much simpler to sit on the sofa and watch a feel-good programme than it is to go out to dinner with your family, but what good is it to do that? We all squander much too much time on pointless activities. It is preferable to create lasting friendships now. There are also millions of lonely people in the world who would kill to have a dinner companion. maximising life's happiness to the fullest. I have to go home, but I have a choice between taking the five-minute subway ride underground or taking a 30-minute leisurely stroll through a park and through streets lined with trees. Living with purpose produces lasting happiness.

*"It isn't what you have, or who you are, or where you are, or what you are doing that makes you happy or unhappy. It is what you think about."-Dale Carnegie*

When we are aroused by things we enjoy, this organic chemical is released. These factors induce short-term happiness because they trigger the release of dopamine in response to a single occurrence. The enjoyment will be lost after this event has ended. Consequently, I classify this as short-term happiness. There is also long-term happiness. Since long-term pleasure is based on other ideas of happiness, it is a little more difficult to express. Feeling content with your life's purpose, your accomplishments, your triumphs, and/or your identity and self-worth will help you live a long and happy life. Long-term happiness is founded on ideas that aren't brought about by just one thing.

*"We tend to forget that happiness doesn't come as a result of getting something we don't have, but rather of recognizing and appreciating what we do have."-Frederick Keonig*

You'll probably feel unsatisfied and dissatisfied if you copy and paste the goals of someone you admire and like. For instance, Elon Musk, for instance, is accomplishing some amazing things, but if I were in his position, I wouldn't be content. My life's mission is very different from his! I have determined my own life's purpose, and I suggest that you do the same. How do you discover your life's purpose? Therefore, how do you find your purpose?

*"In our lives, change is unavoidable, loss is unavoidable. In the adaptability and ease with which we experience change, lies our happiness and freedom."-Buddha*

Here's how you can't locate it: by spending the entire day on a chair waiting for it to find you. By repeatedly doing the same things, you will not find your purpose. Instead, you discover it by doing and doing (new) things. It's also critical to understand that your career and your life's mission are not the same. Too many individuals search for a profession that may also fulfil their sense of purpose in life. Only a very tiny number of people truly find meaning in their jobs. To shorten a long story Another illustration of a person who has a meaningful life is I was graciously given the opportunity to hear how another individual I've met leads a meaningful life.

*"It's the moments that I stopped just to be, rather than do, that have given me true happiness."-Richard Branson*

One of the most widespread myths about living a meaningful life is that it depends on how much money, power, or position a person has amassed. Even if these "goals" have been accomplished, a void still exists, as if something is missing from their lives. Although everyone is different, living a purposeful life should be based on what their spirit is genuinely yearning for to fill the vacuum. It should not be dependent on what society has prescribed. The capacity and freedom to live your life however you wish to is one of the most magnificent benefits of being a person.

*"Others may know pleasure, but pleasure is not happiness. It has no more importance than a shadow following a man."-Muhammad Ali*

There isn't a prescriptive law or manual that tells people how to have meaningful lives. It is more of a personal guideline on how to live a happy life. In other words, if you aren't living out your soul's calling and doing the things that make you feel whole and loved by yourself, nothing else really counts. The good news is that there are things you can do to promote and strengthen your feeling of purpose in life. That's accurate. It is possible to live purposefully, to pursue your passions, and to connect your life with your values. Reaching within and seeking a more meaningful existence may seem like a challenging endeavour. Despite the fact that this is far from the case, You may start living with purpose and leading a better, more satisfying life by paying attention to this advice.

*"A calm and modest life brings more happiness than the pursuit of success combined with constant restlessness."-Albert Einstein*

Everyone aspires to lead a meaningful life. It's a trait of humanity that stems from our dislike of feeling motionless. We must continue to advance toward a target or objective. Without it, we are less content. However, it's simpler said than done. What does living a life with meaning entail? Living with purpose entails pursuing a significant goal that

aligns with your beliefs and passions and makes you happy.
***"Happiness consists more in small conveniences or pleasures that occur every day, than in great pieces of good fortune that happen but seldom to a man in the course of his life."-Benjamin Franklin***

Finding your mission in life is not always simple, so this is more difficult than it seems. This book explains what you can do right away to discover your mission and get started living it. I've included real-world examples of people who have discovered their purpose and lead meaningful lives. How to have a better body image? We all have varied tastes, which is fortunate given that we are all a variety of sizes and forms. If you want to be more body positive, you need to come to this awareness. An estimated 8 million Americans are thought to have an eating disorder of some kind, yet many of them never obtain a formal diagnosis.

> *Being happy doesn't mean everything is perfect. It means you've decided to look beyond the imperfections.*

We have a complicated relationship with our bodies. The vehicle in which we travel is our body. The picture that people perceive is what it is. Our bodily image represents us inadvertently. And regrettably, we have little control over how other people see our bodies. The way we perceive ourselves in the mirror and how we think other people view us both influence how we feel about our bodies. This article claims that a person with a good body image is at ease with both their appearance and their feelings. Despite the fact that they are not flawless, they accept themselves. They understand that who they are on the inside matters more than who they are on the outside, and this is maybe what matters most. On the other hand, the same article asserts that a person with a poor body image suffers from profound self-unhappiness. For what purpose? for society? Do you believe that these adjustments will bring happiness? Sometimes all we need to find pleasure is to accept ourselves as we are.

*"The happiest people in the world are those who feel absolutely terrific about themselves, and this is the natural outgrowth of accepting total responsibility for every part of their life."-Brian Tracy*

Different types of happiness exist. Not just in how we categorise happiness, but also in how we really feel it. It's crucial to understand how these variations might affect the choices we make on a daily basis and whether we live with or without a purpose. Short-term contentment Happiness in the short term is rather simple to describe. It is based on modest, simple means of enjoyment.

*"Optimism is a happiness magnet. If you stay positive, good things and good people will be drawn to you."-Mary Lou Retton*

People who are interested in finding actual contentment practise when it isn't convenient, in contrast to others who like talking about having a satisfied life. After all, practise is what gives purpose. We frequently feel the need to multitask while we go about our daily lives. For example, we may watch TV or play with our phones while we eat, engage in discussions while working, or perform home chores or other tasks while on the phone with someone. The reason this is an issue, though, is because nothing is ever completed to our satisfaction, and ultimately, we have only ever performed mediocrely on everything.

On the other hand, when we keep our attention on one activity at a time, we complete it entirely before going on to the next one. This not only enables us to perform significantly more admirably, but it also provides us with the chance to experience delight and amazement in even the smallest aspects of our lives. This follows logically from existing in the present moment.

*"Plenty of people miss their share of happiness, not because they never found it, but because they didn't stop to enjoy it."-William Feather*

We won't ever be distracted by anything other than our current condition if we only ever pay attention to one item. We frequently put off making adjustments. We put off starting a new goal until after the holidays, pick up our workout regimen again after our vacation is over, and often establish timelines for when we will start doing so. But if we put off carrying out the goals we've set for ourselves, we are in essence putting off our purpose.

*"If you want to be happy, do not dwell in the past, do not worry about the future, focus on living fully in the present."*
*-Roy T. Bennett,*

Why would we wait for something to happen if it is significant enough to us that it will enable us to achieve our goals for being here? Instead, by making adjustments to our lives now rather than later, we will be better able to achieve our goals. Start changing your diet today with your next meal rather than tomorrow's first meal.

*"Happiness always looks small while you hold it in your hands, but let it go, and you learn at once how big and precious it is."-Maxim Gorky*

Your sadhana is a scientific method for achieving both short-term and long-term wellness. You must purge your thoughts of unneeded clutter if you want your sadhana to be fruitful. You are responsible for cultivating the soil. If you plant a seed on a rock, it won't even start to grow. If you keep accumulating other people's trash, nothing will be able to sprout. Nowadays, most people have too much garbage in their brains to be able to see the enormous potential that is being shown to them. I don't want you to squander your life by being unaware of this option.

*"Happiness is something that comes into our lives through doors we don't even remember leaving open."-Rose Lane*

You may be familiar with the tale of Socrates, who was regarded as being very intelligent even during his lifetime. One day, someone approached him and said, "I want to tell you something about Diogenes." "I have a basic principle," Socrates declared. You must pass your speech through the triple filter no matter what you wish to express. What exactly is this triple filter, the guy enquired? First of all, have you verified the truth of whatever it is you are about to tell me now? asked Socrates. "No," the man replied. I was just informed about this. So it doesn't pass the first filter, Socrates remarked. Is it something nice? This is the second filter. No, just the contrary, and that's why I'm telling you. "So it doesn't pass the second filter either," Socrates remarked. Is there any use for it? "No, I don't believe it's beneficial," the guy said. I just wanted to let you know this. "That indicates it doesn't pass any of the filters," Socrates replied. Keep in mind these three filters: Have they made sure that what they wish to tell you is the whole truth before they disclose it to you? Is it a positive trait in someone? Is it beneficial? You will have a lot of mental room to do beneficial, lovely, and spiritual things if you filter out everything that does not fit these three criteria, from what people want to tell you or what you want to tell someone else.

## *How to Predict People's Behavior Better?*

One of the most prevalent worries people have that might make them perform less confidently is feeling uncertain of how other people will act or react. Perhaps they are late for work and are concerned about what their employer will think. So they experience anxiety or insecurity when they come. Or perhaps they are worried about how their colleagues will respond when they make a recommendation during a meeting, which causes them to be cautious and modest instead. The problem is rarely a lack of knowledge about how the other person will behave. We have the issue of forgetting what we already know. You see, there is a really straightforward method that will enable you to foretell how other people will treat or behave in your presence.

Since we are dealing with people and not robots, you won't always be correct, but this is the method that I have discovered to be the most reliable for predicting future behavior. And this basic fact serves as the technique's foundation. People will act in the same manner as they have in the past. People very rarely alter their behaviour while with others, unless, of course, the dynamics of the connection change. Therefore, it is likely that your employer will act in the same way today if he frequently becomes irate when individuals are late. You shouldn't worry if he typically doesn't become angry about such things, according to probability.

In any case, you may prepare now for how to behave with your manager when you report to work. And having that strategy typically gives us a little more assurance regarding the overall circumstance. Most people respond, "Oh yes, I already knew that," when I explain this, since it is so evident to our rational brain. However, the majority of individuals don't actually do this. They continue to worry about how their buddy, lover, boss, or anyone else will act when something happens rather than just assuming that they will act as they always have and making plans accordingly.

*"Happiness is not in the mere possession of money; it lies in the joy of achievement, in the thrill of creative effort."-Franklin D. Roosevelt*

So, this activity is not difficult. Stop worrying about the future and start remembering the past if you find yourself worrying about how the people in your life will behave or respond to anything. Have you ever encountered them in circumstances like these before? If so, the behaviour they exhibited when they first met you is probably what they'll do this time as well. Regularly put this into practise, and you'll quickly notice that you'll cease worrying about how people will act or treat you. Instead, start making straightforward forecasts that you can plan for when necessary.

## *Happiness is when what you think, what you say, and what you do are in harmony.*

You will constantly be occupied with rubbish if you feed yourself unfiltered knowledge, whether it is someone else's or your own. Never enjoy someone else's troubles by spreading rumours about them. You might decide to refrain from criticising someone while you are not speaking to them directly. Spending time mulling over anything someone said or did is a waste of time. Most of you are not in a mental state where, when you close your eyes, you have no more awareness of the outside world. If such is the case, the best course of action is to exhaust yourself completely, leaving no energy for anything that is not essential for your welfare.

The alternative to boredom, idleness, resentment, or sorrow is to pass away from weariness. You do not have to decrease your activities because you are getting older. You will only be able to accomplish more if you continue doing something with a great deal of energy and engagement. A young cowherd took his cows into the forest one day to graze. A cow there gave birth to a calf. He saw a birth for the first time. To him, it was a marvel that this tiny fragment of life appeared out of nowhere. He took up the calf and embraced it out of profound love and care for it. And as it was unable to walk, he carried it back home on his shoulders. He carried the calf on his shoulders once more the next day as he took his cows to the forest, and he continued to do so every day. The little calf eventually developed into a large bull. The man's strength rose with its weight. All of the residents of the town believed him to be Superman by the time he was seen walking around with a fully grown bull on his shoulders. I want to see those kinds of superpeople everywhere.

*"When one door of happiness closes, another opens, but often we look so long at the closed door that we do not see the one that has been opened for us."-Helen Keller*

You shouldn't restrict your abilities. Let's find the boundary that life imposes. Limiting oneself prevents people from making anything significant. It's crucial that you make the most of your life as possible in all respects. Why waste time on things that aren't important when life is so short? Either you must take action to promote your inner well-being or you must help those around you. Whatever sadhana you perform will be far more successful if you fall asleep as soon as your head hits the pillow, since you've used up all of your energy for the day.

*"There is only one cause of unhappiness: the false beliefs you have in your head, beliefs so widespread, so commonly held, that it never occurs to you to question them."-Anthony de Mello*

Do not waste time mulling over what to do and what to avoid. Your life will become pleasant, and travelling will become simple, if you go from being reluctant to being willing, from being inert to being effervescent. And you'll realise that you led a remarkable life when you look back after you pass away. I consider it very crucial that this occurs for you. Be extraordinary and shine a light on the world. You and I will both burn. There are two methods for dealing with your life. Setting and pursuing goals is one strategy. What sort of objectives will you set? Something about the world that you find impressive, something you haven't done yet, or something that hasn't happened yet in your life. You're making an effort to act or seem like someone else, or to follow their lead. Whatever objectives you choose, they are all somewhat constrained by what you already know, or perhaps just somewhat exaggerated versions of it. Is it not sad to attempt to accomplish something you already know for an entire year? My goal is for things to happen to you that you are unaware of.

*"It's fine to decide not to decide about something. You just need a decide-not-to-decide system to get it off your mind." -David Allen*

Things should come into your life that you never could have anticipated. Your life won't be completely enhanced till then. Why limit yourself to what you already know how to do? Simply state that at the end of the day, you must be a little happier, a little more improved, and a little better than when you made objectives for the entire year. This will not succeed as a goal; it is preferable to consider it in hindsight. Tomorrow evening, just ask yourself, "Am I a bit better than yesterday?" Simply taking a glance at these twenty-four hours can increase your awareness. You're not supposed to feel happy or at ease about this. You should be aware of as many facets of your life as possible.

*"We begin from the recognition that all beings cherish happiness and do not want suffering. It then becomes both morally wrong and pragmatically unwise to pursue only one's own happiness oblivious to the feelings and aspirations of all others who surround us as members of the same human family. The wiser course is to think of others when pursuing our own happiness."-Dalai Lama*

## *The secret to inner serenity is healthy emotional flow.*

Every aspect of your life, including how you see and express the world and yourself, will alter when you are essentially joyful and do not need to do anything to be happy. You won't have any vested interests anymore since you will already be joyful by nature, regardless of what you do or don't do, what you receive or don't get, what occurs or doesn't happen.

*"If you are depressed you are living in the past if you are anxious you are living in the future, if you are at peace, you are living in the present." —Lao Tzu*

When you are naturally joyful, everything you do will change significantly. The first and most important duty of a person is to develop into a joyful being. The most important thing in life is not to be happy. It is a basic component of life. What else can you do with your life if you're not happy? Only when you are content will big opportunities present themselves.

*"Do not let the behavior of others destroy your inner peace." -Dalai Lama*

You will only spread your inner excellence through all you do. It doesn't matter how you feel about it; that is the truth. You cannot contribute significantly to the world until something of actual significance occurs within you. Therefore, the first thing you must do if you are worried about the world is to change into a joyful being.

*"Nobody can bring you peace but yourself." -Ralph Waldo Emerson*

No matter what you are chasing in life—whether it's money, influence, education, or service—you are doing it because you have a deep-seated belief that it will make you happy. Because it is our innate nature, every action we take in this world stems from a desire to be happy. You were just content when you were a youngster. That is who you are. You are the source of your own joy, and you can control it.

*"You should feel beautiful and you should feel safe. What you surround yourself with should bring you peace of mind and peace of spirit." -Stacy London*

Live for your family, not for your legacy. The creation of a legacy is ineffective as a goal. Generations tend to remember those who put their family before themselves. Discover your passion. Howard Thurman, a philosopher, once stated, "Don't inquire what the world needs. Find out what gives you life, then go do it. People who have come alive are what the world needs. Put off immediate enjoyment in favour of long-term fulfilment.

*"It isn't enough to talk about peace. One must believe in it. And it isn't enough to believe in it. One must work at it." -Eleanor Roosevelt*

We put a lot of effort into teaching this to our kids, but after that, we stop applying the lesson to ourselves. Is it truly worth going into debt now for a $50,000 automobile if it means you won't have the money for your son's education tomorrow? Do you value the joy of a well-timed sarcastic jab more than the potential damage it can do to a relationship? Is this one-night stand a suitable replacement for a lifetime of dedication? to bolster other individuals.

*"Peace is a daily, a weekly, a monthly process, gradually changing opinions, slowly eroding old barriers, quietly building new structures." -John F. Kennedy*

Did you notice how beautifully the sun rose this morning? The flowers grew, no stars fell, and the galaxies are in excellent working order. Every detail is in place. Even when everything in the universe is working out splendidly today, a single idea that keeps running through your brain causes you to think that everything is going wrong. The main reason why suffering exists is that the majority of people no longer understand what this life is all about. To put it bluntly, you have elevated your little product above the work of the Creator by making their psychological process far more significant than their existential process.

*"Peace is a journey of a thousand miles and it must be taken one step at a time." -Lyndon B. Johnson*

The main cause of all this pain is that The full meaning of what it means to be alive here has escaped us.Your current experience is a result of a thought you are currently having or an emotion you are currently experiencing. Additionally, your thoughts and feelings might not even be related to the constrained reality of your life. The production as a whole is going great, yet one one idea or feeling has the power to wreck the whole thing.

*"Peace brings with it so many positive emotions that it is worth aiming for in all circumstances." -Estella Eliot*

Every day, ask yourself, "What can I do to inspire my wife, my children, my coworkers, my friends, etc." Be a person of honour. What's superior to money? Your standing What lasts longer than fame? Your honesty What is more likely to be discussed in the future than how awesome your automobile was? The dignity and honour of the person, who, for all they know, may have ridden a bus to work every day. Instead of focusing on receiving, live your life by giving. To be remembered, you don't have to be a wealthy benefactor with your name on a wall. Give what you have; do what you can.

*" Peace cannot be kept by force. It can only be achieved by understanding." -Albert Einstein*

Many famous businesspeople, like Bill Gates, Steve Jobs, and Marc Zuckerberg, succeeded at a relatively young age. Although you would believe they were handed a magic formula for success, the fact is that they gave up something in order to be successful. In truth, success requires a lot of sacrifices. It's hardly news that excellence necessitates sacrifice. Any thriving businessman will tell you that getting to the top isn't an easy journey taken in a plush Porsche. Instead, there are things you must give up in order to have a better future, which frequently involves losing your girlfriend or your BMW.

*"Imagine all the people living life in peace. You may say that I'm a dreamer, but I'm not the only one. I hope someday you'll join us and the world will be as one." —John Lennon*

Make your social media feeds uplifting and joyful. Once you've finished unfollowing those bad influencers, go on to find some good ones. Look around to see if you can find any influencers who are doing something that you would truly support. Follow organisations, causes, and activists working to advance body positivity, sustainability, equality, and other causes.

Make sure your feed is balanced between things that will make you feel better or give you more confidence and ones that will motivate you to improve yourself or the world. Set time limits for using social media.

You shouldn't spend hours reading over your social media pages just because they are now encouraging spaces. It's time to start comparing using social media to eating processed food or engaging in harmful habits in general.

*"Peace is not absence of conflict, it is the ability to handle conflict by peaceful means." —Ronald Reagan*

What you refer to as "my mind" is not genuinely yours. You lack independent thought. Please take a close look. What you refer to as "my thoughts" is only the trash heap of civilization. Every person who passes you in the street shoves something into your skull. You actually don't have a choice in terms of who you choose to receive from and who you don't. You will get a lot more from someone if you tell them, "I don't like this individual," than from anybody else. Really, there isn't much of a choice. This trash is helpful if you know how to process and use it.

*"Not one of us can rest, be happy, be at home, be at peace with ourselves, until we end hatred and division."*
*-John Lewis*

You can only use this collection of perceptions and knowledge to help you survive in the world. Nothing is connected to what you are. As I just said, you simply have to realise that your thoughts and feelings are unimportant if you wish to enter into existential reality. Reality has nothing to do with what you believe. It doesn't really apply to daily life. The mind is simply babbling unfounded information that you have learned elsewhere. If you believe it to be significant, you won't search elsewhere. Your focus will naturally go toward whatever you value most. Your entire attention will be focused there if your thoughts and feelings are significant. That, however, is a psychological fact. That is unrelated to anything existential.

*"When you make peace with yourself, you make peace with the world." -Maha Ghosananda*

While occasionally indulging in fatty or sugary foods is acceptable, eating them for three meals a day, every day, will be detrimental to your physical health. Similar to this, see social media as something that should be used sparingly to avoid damaging your mental health. Stop spending time with people who bring you down or limit you.

*"Love and peace of mind do protect us. They allow us to overcome the problems that life hands us. They teach us to survive... to live now... to have the courage to confront each day." -Bernie Siegel*

Nowadays, social media plays a significant role in many of our lives, but the actual people you spend time with are far more significant. Or they ought to be, really. Make a choice to spend less time with people who are a bad influence in your life, who are always depressing you or preventing you from reaching your potential. If your efforts to talk with them about it have met with resistance, While you shouldn't desert a friend who is going through a difficult time, it's definitely a good idea to rethink how much time you spend with individuals who routinely affect you negatively.

*"To seek out your own inner Peace is the greatest gift you could ever hope to give to this world." – Eric Walton*

Generous lives leave enduring imprints on history. Be genuine. Talk honestly with your husband, open up to your kids, and be open with your friends. Men who erect barriers around their hearts and souls are forgotten because no one has ever met them. narrates the tales. If we won't allow ourselves to be recognised, how can we hope to be remembered? Cherish your family. Do you think this is a no-brainer? Well, a lot of us could benefit from a love primer. It is not rude, self-centered, irritable, or keeps track of wrongdoings.

*"Inner peace can be reached only when we practice forgiveness. Forgiveness is letting go of the past, and is therefore the means for correcting our misperceptions."*
*-Gerald G. Jampolsky*

Love rejoices in the truth rather than taking pleasure in wickedness. It always defends, always believes, always aspires, and always endures. Create a celebration-focused culture in your household. Be like the family who celebrates the 100th anniversary of their great-grandparents' arrival in America or the couple who sends cards to each other on the occasion of their first date, engagement, or closing on their first house.

*"You'll never find peace of mind until you listen to your heart." -George Michael*

Be the family that commemorates milestones, anniversaries, memories, and historical events. "Be a champion for what you believe in, and then let your convictions direct your course of action." Find a mistake and fix it. Perhaps your truly big contribution is still to come. Become an advocate for your beliefs, and then let them direct your course of action. The unexamined existence, according to Socrates, is not worth living. Perhaps as a result of some introspection, your legacy will become apparent.

*"Having inner peace means committing to letting go of self-criticism and self-doubt."-Sanaya Roman*

Millions of people who slept yesterday are still asleep today, while you and I are still awake. Isn't it wonderful that you're awake? So be happy that you got up. Next, take a peek around, and if you see somebody, give them a grin. Someone close to so many people did not get out of bed this morning. Wow! Everyone you care about woke up. Isn't today wonderful? Then step outside and observe the trees. Last night, they also did not pass away.

*"Mindset is everything. Like the eye of a storm -find the sunshine and calm within you, even if there is chaos outside of you." -Brittany Burgunder*

Although you may find this absurd, you will understand its truth when a loved one fails to awaken. Don't wait till then to appreciate its worth. Knowing that you are alive and that everything that matters to you is alive is the most valuable thing. It is not anything absurd. So many people did not wake up on this terrible night, including the loved ones of so many others. Isn't it a wonderful occasion? At least smile and express appreciation. Get better at loving a few people.

*"Life is a series of natural and spontaneous changes. Don't resist them; that only creates sorrow. Let reality be reality. Let things flow naturally forward in whatever way they like." -Lao Tzu*

Today, we are pursuing happiness with such fervour that the planet's basic existence is in danger. Don't try to find happiness. Understand how to share your delight with others. When you look back on your life, the most beautiful times in it are when you are experiencing joy, not when you are trying to find it. Your quality will never be what you save. Your quality is seen in what you give out. If you hold on to your happiness, nobody will hold you accountable after you pass away. The first thing you should do when you get up is smile. To whom? No one. Because it's not a minor thing that you woke up at all.

*"The life of inner peace, being harmonious and without stress, is the easiest type of existence." —Norman Vincent Peale*

It is not based on what you possess. Depending on how they are at the time. The majority of people suffer, not because of what they lack. Simply said, it's because they are making comparisons between themselves and others. You make yourself sad because you are riding a motorcycle and you notice someone driving a Mercedes. He sees you on a motorcycle and thinks of it as a limousine for a person on a bicycle. When someone sees the bicycle while strolling down the street, they may think, "Wow, what I would have done with my life if I simply had that!" It is a pointless game that never ends.

*"Each one has to find his peace from within. And peace to be real must be unaffected by outside circumstances." — Mahatma Gandhi*

The way you dress, your educational background, your family history, or the amount of money you have in the bank right now do not affect the quality of your life. The quality of your life is determined by how content and joyful you are from within. All those individuals will never experience genuine joy in their life since they rely on other people's actions to make them happy. It is surely time for us to examine how to cultivate our own wellness.

*"When you've seen beyond yourself, then you may find, peace of mind is waiting there." – George Harrison*

You can plainly understand from your own life experience that altering your interiority is the only way for you to truly find wellbeing. If you rely on the outside world to make you happy, you need to realise that things outside of your control rarely go exactly as you would like them to. When this is the case, at least one person—you—must have your desires fulfilled. The obvious answer would be delight if things turned out the way you wanted them to. There is no doubt that someone who lacks food and other essentials for living may suffer physically. That requires attention. We must address such issues first for these individuals. However, the majority of people have a never-ending list of requirements. Do you believe the person operating the vehicle is happier than the person crossing the street? You're under no obligation to pursue that. Joy is the only state you can be in if you revert to your true nature.

*"You have to grow from the inside out. None can teach you, none can make you spiritual. There is no other teacher but your own soul." -Swami Vivekananda*

## *Find your purpose and unlock your best life.*

The word "purpose" is frequently misused. I've observed a lot of individuals searching for a higher meaning in life, such as a type of world-saving mission. Basically, they were looking for something to satisfy their egos and make them feel really exceptional. The concept of "purpose" is distinct. You don't have to make the world better. It's simply a matter of changing your focus from "what you can take from life today" to "how you can contribute to life today." That's my list, then.

*"Our prime purpose in this life is to help others. And if you can't help them, at least don't hurt them."- Dalai Lama*

What do we define as the purpose of our lives? Purpose must begin with each of us as an individual. What is the mission we see for ourselves? Let's start by discussing purpose in terms of human psychology. While some could contend that each of us has a distinct mission, the bulk of us have two characteristics and will identify with them. Development is the first. Being the best version of ourselves is our top priority as humans, along with actualizing our potential and growing to our fullest potential.

*"I truly believe that everything that we do and everyone that we meet is put in our path for a purpose. There are no accidents; we're all teachers - if we're willing to pay attention to the lessons we learn, trust our positive instincts and not be afraid to take risks or wait for some miracle to come knocking at our door." -Marla Gibbs*

Millions of species, 30,000 distinct varieties of life, and over 7 billion people all cohabit and provide for one another on Earth in their own unique ways. It's incredible how much is out there that we don't know and that has to be discovered. As long as you are in this world, keep embracing life. Only in this way can we continue to exist. Consider others. Giving back to the community is a wonderful way to give life purpose again, which might frequently feel like it's going downhill otherwise.

*"True happiness is not attained through self-gratification, but through fidelity to a worthy purpose."- Helen Keller*

There are countless ways to help others, such as maintaining an elderly neighbor's garden or volunteering at a local charity shop. Yes, you are performing this labour gratuitously and for complete strangers, but someone's day will suddenly be made better because of your kindness.

Giving back is the most fulfilling thing you can do.

People who are only interested in making money for themselves will typically find that their pursuit of pleasure or collecting material possessions delivers a declining sense of fulfilment, and life will become meaningless and dull. Our ambition to develop our purpose must be grounded in a genuine desire to act morally. We will be met with cynicism and scepticism if our activities are seen as just another effort to persuade our staff to be more productive or profitable.

*"The purpose of human life is to serve, and to show compassion and the will to help others."- Albert Schweitzer*

The notion that everything happens in life for a reason lies at the very core of a life lived with purpose. The purpose of adversity is to teach us the lessons we need to know in order to advance. When something doesn't work out the way we expected it to, it's because we weren't ready for the new chance that came along. When we keep our attention solely on the present, we only have an impact on the aspects of the world that we have the power to alter. Do not let dogma, which is living according to the conclusions of other people's thinking, capture you. Keep your inner voice from being drowned out by the clamour of other people's thoughts. The most essential thing to remember is to have the guts to listen to your heart and intuition because they somehow already know who you are meant to be. "Everything else is just a side note." Apple Inc.

- Right now, how do you feel about your life?
- Do you experience daily elation?
- Do you look forward to the next event with anticipation?

Purposeful describes the steps to help you live a full life—a life of purpose, direction, and meaning—whatever that is for you. It includes action guides and activities. It's about becoming the kind of person you want to be and living the kind of life you want to live. If they don't have a plan for their time on earth, they will never be prolific and a blessing to their family, society, nation, and generations. The majority of individuals have a routine existence that involves getting up in the morning, going after money, returning home, eating, drinking, and engaging in sexual activity, and repeating the cycle until death arrives and takes man away.

*"Everyone has a purpose in life and a unique talent to give to others. And when we blend this unique talent with service to others, we experience the ecstasy and exultation of own spirit, which is the ultimate goal of all goals."*
*-Kallam Anji Reddy*

Our eagerness to trust life outweighs our capacity for reason as long as we maintain this awareness. So, effortless living is the readiness to let go of our urge for desired results and accept the flow experience. We release situations that no longer benefit us rather than frantically grasping at life. To let go means to mentally and emotionally distance oneself from circumstances that are out of our control. Instead of moving with the flow, energy is wasted fighting against life. The egoic mind asserts that it is far more intelligent than that which directs the stars and planets. Given that we are a minor component in a carefully planned process, we are aware of the fallacy of that assumption.

*"When you're surrounded by people who share a passionate commitment around a common purpose, anything is possible."- Howard Schultz*

The Almighty never acts haphazardly; he gave everything, including people, a reason when he created it. According to the Bhagvad Gita, the Almighty created man and assigned him to live on this earth for the primary purpose of creation. The Man was to rule over the earth by procreating, multiplying, and replenishing it.

*"The purpose of life is not to be happy. It is to be useful, to be honourable, to be compassionate, to have it make some difference that you have lived and lived well." — Ralph Waldo Emerson*

Before giving birth to man, almighty, a loving and principled father, created everything that man would need to enjoy life. However, he also established rules by which men must carry out their responsibilities as rulers. Finding one's life's purpose has, for many people, become an illusion. Yet there are guidelines for leading a meaningful life that, when followed, will lead to people bearing fruit and becoming blessings. Although unwanted pregnancies are possible, no one's existence on earth is intended to be in vain. Every person on earth has a purpose that almighty has for them; a purpose that, even if they are unaware of it, requires them to produce fruit and be of benefit.

*"Your work is going to fill a large part of your life, and the only way to be truly satisfied is to do what you believe is great work. And the only way to do great work is to love what you do. If you haven't found it yet, keep looking. Don't settle. As with all matters of the heart, you'll know when you find it." — Steve Jobs*

The desire for a feeling of purpose has long been acknowledged as a fundamental human need and a significant source of motivation in life. It is said that purpose is to the soul what air is to our lungs. We find hope and optimism in purpose. It encourages a favourable attitude and an innate drive for whatever we are doing or seeking. What purpose is to our soul, breath is to our lungs. When a person has a clear sense of goal and that objective is engrained in his or her culture, it has a profoundly transformative effect on an individual. It boosts people's productivity and promotes appropriate behaviour that serves that goal. Additionally, it helps the business connect emotionally with its clientele. Let's examine each one separately.

*"The purpose of life is undoubtedly to know oneself. We can't do it unless we learn to identify with everything that lives. The instrument of this knowledge is boundless, selfless service."- Mahatma Gandhi*

When you discover how to live a more purposeful life, you stop waiting for better circumstances and start appreciating the present. Instead of basing your happiness on something that may or may not happen in the future, enjoy what is happening around you right now. Keep in mind that you should be glad because you were a part of the beginning of something new rather than unhappy because something has ended.

*"The purpose of life, after all, is to live it, to taste experience to the utmost, to reach out eagerly and without fear for newer and richer experience." – Eleanor Roosevelt*

Our sorrows are caused by our sinful reactions. Mohandas Karamchand Gandhi, usually referred to as "Mahatma" or the "Great Soul," was an Indian hero and a political and spiritual leader. He adhered to the Hindu faith, as do I. Mahatma Gandhi used nonviolent resistance to win India's freedom. Mahatma Gandhi travelled to South Africa later that year to work there and saw that there was a lot of animosity toward Indians there. He started protesting because of this, and eventually he turned into a beloved figure to millions of people. Mahatma Gandhi is likely the only person, after the Buddha, who gives a measure of man's ability to nurture a rich inner life and achieve self-transformation. His life serves as an example of philosophy as the art of living. After the Buddha, Mahatma Gandhi is likely the only person who offers an indication of how far a person might develop a rich inner life and achieve self-transformation. How much of yourself can you change? How much internal change are you capable of making on your own, without assistance from any outside source, such as a guru?

*"The main purpose of life is to live rightly, think rightly, and act rightly." "The soul must languish when we give all our thoughts to the body." —Mahatma Gandhi*

Mahatma Gandhi is a multifaceted individual who excels as a politician, social reformer, and mass leader. He serves as an example of developing oneself. Before leading the Indian liberation movement, he lived in South Africa to fight injustice and classism. Within ten years, Mahatma Gandhi had spread the Satyagraha school of thought and pushed the nation toward racial and social equality. Mahatma Gandhi had a first-class ticket, so he was placed in the first-class section. Since non-whites and "coolies" (a derogatory name for Indians) were not allowed in first-class compartments, a white individual who entered the cabin hurried to summon the white railway authorities, who ordered Mahatma Gandhi to transfer himself to the van compartment. Mahatma Gandhi objected and provided his ticket, but was told to leave politely or he would be forcibly removed. Mahatma Gandhi was forced out of the train and his luggage was thrown onto the platform when he refused to follow the officer's instructions. He became an activist to defend his rights as a result of this humiliation.

The only Indian who was well-known worldwide was Mahatma Gandhi, who was the first to place India on the map of the world. He was the first Indian to get notoriety in politics, initially outside of India. He was the greatest mass mobilizer in Indian history, bringing millions of people into the public eye, particularly women.

*"What is success? I think it is a mixture of having a flair for the thing that you are doing; knowing that it is not enough, that you have got to have hard work and a certain sense of purpose."-Margaret Thatcher*

For a quarter of a century, Mahatma Gandhi had such power over Indian politics that anybody who incurred his anger risked political suicide. He is the only leader in India, and maybe the whole globe, who has had an impact on so many facets of life and has something to say about each one, whether it be on issues of morality, sexuality, religion, the economy, or high politics.

*"There is one quality which one must possess to win, and that is definiteness of purpose, the knowledge of what one wants, and a burning desire to possess it."- Napoleon Hill*

Being an activist, he created the Satyagraha (truth-force) tactic, in which protesters participated in nonviolent marches and offered themselves up for arrest in opposition to unjust laws. In their early years of resistance to apartheid in South Africa, the African National Congress and the civil rights movement in the United States both benefited from this strategy. He was a thin man with a toothless grin, spectacles, and the traditional Hindu loincloth known as a dhoti. He also walked with a bamboo staff. He had the demeanour of a plain Hindu holy man. Mahatma Gandhi, however, confronted one of the mightiest empires in history with nothing more than remarkable courage and a steadfast dedication to peaceful resistance. Mahatma Gandhi fought against these injustices for 21 years.

*"The only purpose for which power can be rightfully exercised over any member of a civilized community, against his will, is to prevent harm to others. His own good, either physical or moral, is not sufficient warrant."-John Stuart Mill*

Martin Luther King Jr. formed his nonviolent ideology during this time, which held that only nonviolent protests, like boycotts, marches, and sit-ins, could effect change. The American Baptist clergyman was a pioneer in the nation's Civil Rights Movement and a nonviolent campaigner. He organised the Montgomery bus boycott in 1955 and gave the possibly greatest speech in history, "I Have a Dream," in front of more than 250,000 people at the Washington, D.C., Civil Rights March in 1963. Mahatma Gandhi served as an influence on Martin Luther King Jr. when he was chosen to head the Montgomery bus boycott in Alabama in 1955. King would later remark that "India's Gandhi was the guiding light of our approach of nonviolent social change while the Montgomery boycott was ongoing." When the civil rights activist was training to become a minister, he first learned about Gandhi's nonviolent ideology.

*"I refuse to accept the view that mankind is so tragically bound to the starless midnight of racism and war that the bright daybreak of peace and brotherhood can never become a reality... I believe that unarmed truth and unconditional love will have the final word."-Martin Luther King Jr.*

King claimed that Gandhi provided him with "the way of social transformation I had been seeking" because of his capacity to effect change via love and nonviolence. King and his wife, Coretta Scott, King came to India after the boycott, which saw black residents of Montgomery refuse to board public transportation in an effort to denounce segregated seating, was successful. They visited the Gandhi family, even though Gandhi had already been slain at that point. When King returned to the United States, he continued to struggle for African Americans' equal rights using Gandhi's nonviolent tactics. Gandhi battled evil with the same zeal and strength as the violent resisters, but he did so out of love rather than hatred, according to King.

*"We must develop and maintain the capacity to forgive. He who is devoid of the power to forgive is devoid of the power to love. There is some good in the worst of us and some evil in the best of us. When we discover this, we are less prone to hate our enemies."-Martin Luther King Jr.*

Gandhi's Satyagraha campaign served as an inspiration for Mandela. It was a potent demonstration of passive resistance to injustice. This later served as motivation for the creation of the African National Congress and reaffirmed Mandela's faith in the universality of mankind. Mandela, who is sometimes referred to as the "Gandhi of South Africa," had close ties to India and traits in common with that country's "Father of the Nation." He was so impressed by Gandhi that he attributed Gandhi's philosophy to the success of South Africa's truth and reconciliation committee.

*"What our origins are doesn't matter. What counts is where our qualities enable us to arrive."-Nelson Mandela*

Nelson Mandela a powerful voice of protest against injustice, a Gandhian at heart, a born leader for the underprivileged, a spirit of revolt against prejudice, and a warrior against the apartheid system, is a prime example of this. It would be pointless to attempt to summarise Nelson Mandela's life in an essay because it is so full of significant events. He is frequently referred to as the Mahatma Gandhi of South Africa because of his Gandhian-inspired human principles. Despite not having any roots in India, he had a close political relationship with Gandhi and the country. The Indian Eagle puts in a little effort to explore his relations with India and the Mahatma.

*"There is no easy walk to freedom anywhere, and many of us will have to pass through the valley of the shadow of death again and again before we reach the mountaintop of our desires."- Nelson Mandela*

Nelson Mandela was a revolutionary against apartheid who devoted his youth to the cause of African equality.He was imprisoned on Robben Island for life following violent protests, but was eventually released 27 years later. He spread lessons of forgiveness and equality after being freed. Mandela received the Nobel Peace Prize in 1993, and one year later he was elected as South Africa's first black president. Apartheid was finally ended in 1991.

*"I learned that courage was not the absence of fear, but the triumph over it." – Nelson Mandela*

One of the motivating factors behind Nelson Mandela's lifetime anti-apartheid fight was the Gandhian ideology. He looked up to Mahatma Gandhi as a leader. He was a devoted adherent of Gandhi's teachings on nonviolence and truth. Soon after his release from prison in 1990, he received the Bharat Ratna award. He was the country's highest civilian honor's first non-Indian recipient.

*"I learned that courage was not the absence of fear, but the triumph over it. The brave man is not he who does not feel afraid, but he who conquers that fear."- Nelson Mandela*

By summarising one of Nelson Mandela's remarks on Mahatma Gandhi, we want to demonstrate his passionate commitment to the latter. The Mahatma is an inseparable part of the African history of the movement against racism in South Africa, where he left an indelible influence of his unwavering determination in defiance of the wrong, in support of the right, and in pursuit of justice for the non-white, through his philosophy of truth and nonviolence, he said at the Gandhi Memorial's opening ceremony in South Africa in 1993.

Nelson Mandela maintained a positive relationship with India and Indian officials even after serving up to 27 years in jail for his opposition to the South African government's apartheid policy. For Indians of the twenty-first century, he is a very inspiring and magnificent character, comparable to the great sons of Mother India. Gandhi's teachings had a significant effect on both his political and non-political efforts to ensure peace and justice for black Africans, which earned him the 2001 International Gandhi Peace Prize.

*"Our human compassion binds us the one to the other - not in pity or patronizingly, but as human beings who have learnt how to turn our common suffering into hope for the future."- Nelson Mandela*

Nelson Mandela saw his trip to India as a religious pilgrimage. For this most famous opponent of apartheid, India was a country of principles and values. He visited Ahmedabad, where Gandhi had developed his nonviolent concept after returning to India from South Africa, where he had focused on his self-help ideas. In one of his addresses, Mandela claimed that he would never be able to live up to the standards of humanity, grandeur, and simplicity that the Mahatma had set through his own life's examples.

*"Our prime purpose in this life is to help others. And if you can't help them, at least don't hurt them." -Dalai Lama*

The first and most crucial step in finding the solutions to how to lead a more fulfilling life is to have a clear knowledge of not just what you want your life to look like, but also how you truly want to live it. You are responsible for finding personal happiness, purpose, and satisfaction. Finding your mission in life is similar to discovering anything new. People frequently seek to leap in with both feet when they become aroused. Finding meaning, though, requires more small steps. You will have more time to properly focus on what you want and what you can do to experience a sense of purpose if you go more slowly. As you move on, remember that you can depend on yourself to live each day to the fullest. Finding thankfulness is crucial for living a more fulfilling life, yet it may occasionally be challenging to find gratitude in the things around us. For this reason, it's crucial that you start out small on your path to living a life of meaning.

*"To succeed in your mission, you must have single-minded devotion to your goal." -A. P. J. Abdul Kalam*

You too would see a glimpse of the endless options open to you if you looked through the same eyes. Be aware of the elements in your life to begin where you are. What you now own is the ideal basis for leading a prosperous life. Step away from your thoughts and into the vast ocean of your heart. Listen for the peace and clarity that may be found in the silent silence. The surge of inspiration he mentions is created by the energy and willpower he is referring to. Start from where you are, take the first step with faith, and have confidence that as long as you keep moving ahead, you will be led. Momentum conveys an enormous force that may outweigh difficulty and adversity. Starting from where you are right now, make a conscious decision to go forward with optimism and vigour, certain that life will guide you to where you need to be.

*"Thousands of candles can be lighted from a single candle, and the life of the candle will not be shortened. Happiness never decreases by being shared." -Buddha*

Live in accordance with your values. Understanding what life, and especially your life, should feel like is one of the most crucial aspects of learning how to live a worthwhile existence. It could appear as though you are in a fog when you aren't being the real you. Despite being occupied, boredom still exists. You're rested, yet you're constantly worn out. Furthermore, even the smallest duties seem like an impossible burden. Living with purpose entails acting in accordance with your views and values and in a way that is consistent with how you feel. Although leading a purposeful life won't always result in a higher income, it will increase your desire to be a part of something greater than yourself. And the prize for doing so is inestimable.

*"Outstanding people have one thing in common: an absolute sense of mission." -Zig Ziglar*

Setting mission has long been acknowledged as a potent strategy for raising our performance or behaviour. It may be quite effective in launching and directing us along a more meaningful and rewarding road when we apply the same method to discovering objectives for our own life. Knowing what you truly want to accomplish in life may often be the hardest part of setting life goals. We may have hazy concepts or just be unsure of where to go for them. But having attainable and meaningful life objectives may help us get a new perspective and, more significantly, can make us happier and more pleased with our lives. The desirable states that people want to achieve, maintain, or avoid are known as life goals. Simply expressed, these objectives are things we wish to achieve or complete in our life. They are usually more significant and connected to our true selves.

*"By letting it go it all gets done. The world is won by those who let it go. But when you try and try, the world is beyond winning." — Lao Tzu*

Any initiative to forge a bond of purpose must be grounded on a social contract of faith in our people. Any drive for purpose will be seen as just another paper exercise, or worse, a cunning strategy to use our people as a means to an end without the society ultimately caring about them as people, if we have not consistently communicated that we care and that our people matter, and if we have not acted in a way that is consistent with this. Such actions will only serve to further dehumanise our staff members and distance them from our goal of establishing a feeling of community.On the other hand, if our actions are perceived as coming from a leadership that genuinely cares about acting in the best interests of its employees and the business, it will inspire a wave of goodwill that will advance us toward our shared goal of fulfilling that shared purpose.

*"A mission statement is not something you write overnight... But fundamentally, your mission statement becomes your constitution, the solid expression of your vision and values. It becomes the criterion by which you measure everything else in your life. " -Stephen Covey*

*Your moral compass define who you are.*

In a world full of uncertainty, no one can guarantee tomorrow. I wanted my readers or students to have a set of guiding principles because I was inspired by the birth of my children. I wanted children to be aware of our family's values at all times. In this age of growing connectivity and technology, fewer and fewer individuals have their own moral compass. There is a constant barrage of media that aims to grab our attention and instil terror in our thoughts. This book is not restricted to parents of young children. All families or people who want to create their own legacy should do this. You may start by setting a purpose, making the required preparations, and writing down your rules for living.

> ***"Peace of mind produces right values, right values produce right thoughts. Right thoughts produce right actions."-Mark Richardson***

A moral compass is a clear feeling of integrity and the will to act morally. When making decisions in life, everyone of us is influenced by our moral compass and conscience. Your character will constantly be strengthened by doing this, making you a person of great worth and ideals.There are certain people, nevertheless, who lack this moral compass and engage in unethical behaviour. But you should always possess the guts to act morally.You will always find success and peace of mind if your moral compass and conscience are clear in all aspects of your life—personal, professional, and workplace.

> ***"The biggest challenge, I think, is always maintaining your moral compass." -Barack Obama***

After reading this book, take the first step if you want to start anything new. Start right away to avoid missing out on your chance to achieve your goals. When we're not paying attention to the here and now, what are we thinking about? Either we are lamenting the past or we are fearing the future. Will lamenting the past, however, alter the circumstances? Can we exert influence over something that hasn't even happened yet? Naturally, because the answer to both of those questions is "no," the only thing left to worry about is the present.

*"When values, thoughts, feelings, and actions are in alignment, a person becomes focused and character is strengthened."-John C. Maxwell*

How to improve your life? Are you ready to improve yourself? No Comparative Because of social media, we've developed a strong habit of contrasting our lives with those of others. Everyone else's life seems so perfect; why can't mine? Self-talk like this needs to cease. You need to quit worrying so much about what other people are doing and start concentrating on your own particular ambitions if you want to truly enjoy life.

*"I have learned that as long as I hold fast to my beliefs and values, and follow my own moral compass, then the only expectations I need to live up to are my own."*
*-Michelle Obama*

Being selfish once in a while is not harmful. Take a break from the screen and spend some "me time." Being Present Because it's so crucial, people frequently say to "live in the moment." The amazing things that are taking place right now are being overlooked because we are either too preoccupied with remembering the past or planning the future. When you squander time wishing it away or daydreaming about events that happened in the past, time goes by very quickly. Try to focus as much of your attention as you can on being in the present moment. Yoga is the ideal way to begin to practise mindfulness.

*"Good values are like a magnet – they attract good people."-John Wooden*

Show your appreciation In order to truly maximise your life, self-reflection is essential. Sometimes it's necessary to remind ourselves of all the great things we have to be thankful for since we often focus more on what we don't have than what we do. Maybe you have a terrific group of friends or a job you enjoy. Make an effort to reflect. If necessary, start a gratitude journal and write down three things each day for which you are grateful. It's a great tool for perspective-setting since it may make what seemed like a terrible day not so horrible after all.

***"Your core values are the deeply held beliefs that authentically describe your soul."-John C. Maxwell***

We understand that you're busy, hungry, and sleepy. But doing as much exercise as you can each day can improve your mood significantly. It not only encourages greater health, but it also makes you stronger and more fit for upcoming excursions. The hardest thing is getting started; after you've done that, the muscle-toning endorphin surges continue nonstop.

***"Define your priorities, know your values and believe in your purpose. Only then can you effectively share yourself with others."-Les Brown***

We do our best to remain in our growth zone, though. That mysterious space between our comfort zone and our panic zone is our growth zone. It's where we develop as people, and it doesn't just involve getting better at what we're doing; it also teaches us courage and self-assurance when we discover that we can perform tasks successfully even when we don't feel entirely at ease or confident doing them. Because being confident doesn't mean you're free of anxiety, tension, or any other negative emotion. Once Ralph Marston said, "Live your days on the positive side of life, in tune with your most treasured values. And in each moment you'll have much to live for."

Confident means knowing that you can carry out your obligations despite the presence of those emotions. Though somewhat less frequently than others, these emotions are nonetheless felt by the most self-assured individuals. And when they do, they make sure that those feelings don't keep them back by employing the same techniques that you're about to discover.

*"Values reflect what is important to the way you live and work."- Anonymous*

You can only truly possess confidence if you realise that anxiety or tension won't prevent you from carrying out your goals and duties, any more than a slight morning hangover will prevent you from attending work or school. Maintain your whole commitment to the idea and continue to nourish and fertilise it through activities as and when the mood strikes. This will prevent possible blockages from occurring by keeping you in your flow rather than placing you under excessive pressure.

*"Achievement of your happiness is the only moral purpose of your life, and that happiness, not pain or mindless self-indulgence, is the proof of your moral integrity, since it is the proof and the result of your loyalty to the achievement of your values."-Ayn Rand*

We need to understand the distinction between stressful and traumatic experiences in order to determine what is in our growth zone. Because stress is not only beneficial when attempting to grow, it is also required. I suppose trauma should be avoided. Again, when I refer to trauma, I mean anything that makes us want to hide away, run away, vomit, or cry. This is your reflex to fight, flee, or freeze. Typically, you will either feel extremely irritated and angry, physically flee the situation, or utterly freeze and lose all ability to think, act, or speak. You are in your panic zone at this point. If it does, go back and reconsider what you had planned to do.

*"Apart from values and ethics which I have tried to live by, the legacy I would like to leave behind is a very simple one - that I have always stood up for what I consider to be the right thing, and I have tried to be as fair and equitable as I could be."- Ratan Tata*

Do you ever feel like you should have accomplished more in life? You can have the overpowering impression that, from where you are right now, you will never get to your objective. Please allow me to allay your concerns. As long as you decide to move forward resolutely, you are in a good position to take any course. When you lose touch with your authentic self, tension develops. An inner voice that won't be pleased until it gets what it wants only serves to exacerbate this. I refer to it as the inner critic, which rules your mental process and is ingrained from an early age.

*"If we are to go forward, we must go back and rediscover those precious values - that all reality hinges on moral foundations and that all reality has spiritual control."-Martin Luther King, Jr.*

No matter how fulfilling you think your life is, there's always somewhere else you want to be. You never feel content because your ego always tells you to chase your next goal in order to find happiness. Do you have that feeling? Is it true that you are sad and want something better—a better relationship, a better financial situation, a better job, or more material possessions? However, when they do, you are only momentarily content. The thrill soon wears off, and you go out in search of the next adventure to keep you engrossed.

*"Values are like fingerprints. Nobodies are the same but you leave them all over everything you do."-Elvis Presley*

I compare it to the scurrying white rabbit from the Alice in Wonderland story, who keeps checking his pocket watch and saying, "Oh dear! I'm sorry! I'll arrive too late! Moving from one place to another without stopping to recognise your accomplishments gives you that impression. Instead of living your life, you're eluding it by avoiding seeing reality as it is.

*"Just as your car runs more smoothly and requires less energy to go faster and farther when the wheels are in perfect alignment, you perform better when your thoughts, feelings, emotions, goals, and values are in balance."- Brian Tracy*

Because you naively follow a goal without understanding the motivations behind it, this results in a barren existence.It appears as though you are attempting to control the future as you envision it. Everyone is aware that life rarely goes as expected. Your well-crafted plans will inevitably be derailed by diversions and roadblocks.

## Set out your daily activities so that time works for you rather than against you.

If you go from one goal to another without applying what you've learned, you miss out on important life lessons. Years later, you regret the fantastic possibilities that you missed while living your best life. Everyone has a unique calling or purpose in life, and each person is tasked with completing a certain task. Because of this, neither his life nor his replacement are possible. As a result, each person's work and the opportunity to complete it are distinct. To be present to what is happening, it is necessary to perceive life in the context of the larger picture.

*"Wherever I go meeting the public... spreading a message of human values, spreading a message of harmony, is the most important thing."- Dalai Lama*

You miss out on the essential lessons woven into your trip if you categorise every encounter as good or negative. Life is a series of gifts, but only if you choose to use them. Starting where you are means appreciating your existing situation. To live a life with meaning, you don't need to have all the knowledge, money, or ideal circumstances. What is needed is a dedication to making baby steps ahead while trusting that the road will become clear as long as you have a clear intention.

According to research by United Healthcare, 93% of volunteers reported feeling happy as a consequence. Additionally, 88% reported higher self-esteem. 85% of people who volunteered made new acquaintances. 79% had less stress. Make an action plan for your objectives and put them into action! It has a list of things to complete before passing away. Then set out to accomplish them. Always consider your actions, and only carry them out if they have a purpose.

*"Our morality is based on so many factors: of where we were born, who we were born to, what values were instilled in us, what values we chose, the way that our lives have shaped us. That dictates so much of what we assume is our morality, and also the culture, all of these things."- Oscar Isaac*

Our thoughts shut off as a result of boredom and restlessness, and we become more docile. Let's not deceive ourselves; neither your history nor your future are shaped by it, any more than the weather last week predicts the weather five years from now. Given your degree of knowledge, your history has brought you to this location in time. Because you prioritise personal development, you are reading this, which is an indication of advancement. There will definitely be diversions, setbacks, difficulties, and failures along your life's road.

*"It was character that got us out of bed, commitment that moved us into action, and discipline that enabled us to follow through."- Zig Ziglar*

Other than the certainty that you can realise your full potential, nothing is definite. Regardless of what we experience, living with purpose can help us be more resilient and perhaps even grow. Because they struggle with false ideas about how life should be, the majority of individuals play the game of life while pinned to the ropes. This is a surefire prescription for failure since your ideas about life don't actually make it happen; instead, they only generate agony and unhappiness.

*"The right moral compass is trying hard to think about what customers want."-Sundar Pichai*

Instead, I'm content because I was able to put a lot of effort into things that gave me a sense of purpose and because I was able to accomplish things that made me extremely proud. As a result, without depending on specific occurrences, I have established a condition in which I am content by default. I believe that my intentional way of living has contributed to some of this. A happy life is one that has a purpose.

*"The men can have a moral compass that is just unshakeable, they can have ethics that run to the core."*
*-Lupe Fiasco*

You have considerably more influence over your long-term satisfaction when you live your life with a purpose. You won't feel like you're working toward some nebulous objective that doesn't make you happy while merely floating along. Your long-term enjoyment, fulfilment, and sense of accomplishment are much easier to define when you have a purpose. You can guide your life in the most beneficial way when you have a purpose. And it is along that path that you may find lasting happiness!

*"Real integrity is doing the right thing, knowing that nobody's going to know whether you did it or not." -Oprah Winfrey*

Many of us unconsciously use social media to divert our attention when we're feeling bad. Perhaps you were hoping I'd suggest you shouldn't do this at all. However, research has indicated a highly variable impact of social media use on wellbeing. Some claim it enhances wellbeing, while others claim the reverse. One piece of research in particular provides a plausible explanation: how you feel about social media is more important than how you use it.

*"If people use common sense and their own guiding moral compass, I think they'll generally stay out of trouble."-Steve Chabot*

Utilising the network increases your sense of wellbeing and self-worth if you feel an emotional connection to it and it is a part of your everyday life. Therefore, it probably won't assist you if you're logging in for the first time in a month and you can't even remember who you're linked to. However, there isn't really anything wrong with using it to make you feel like a member of a community.

Never be hesitant to stop doing things that aren't helping you on your journey. It would be a waste of life to do anything else. Don't do anything if you don't enjoy it. Spend your time and effort on activities that make you happy and fulfilled.

What makes you so angry? Find what you enjoy doing by getting out there. Stop doing a job that you find uninteresting. When you're prepared to work it full-time, quit your job. Make your passion into a successful multimillion-dollar enterprise. Make it worth several billions of dollars and even better. Be receptive to criticism but avoid letting it impact you. The goal of criticism is to make you a better person. The glass is either half full or half empty. Why not claim that it is neither?

*"The highest possible stage in moral culture is when we recognize that we ought to control our thoughts." -Charles Darwin*

Actually, it is completely full; the upper half is air and the bottom half is water. Everything is a question of perspective. Adopt perspectives that will help you, not ones that will limit you. You'll be able to live a life that is significantly richer than others if you can always find the bright side of things. If there is something about someone you dislike, tell him or her directly; if not, keep your mouth shut. Speaking ill of others is rude and shows limited thinking. We will always be narrow-minded and exclusive if everyone simply considers their own point of view. Consider the viewpoints of others.

*"The moral compass was only ever a means to an end and the end is survival of the individuals who use it most creatively."- Derek Robertson*

Be courteous and compassionate to everyone you come into contact with. Have confidence in your skills and abilities. Replace your limiting thoughts with empowering ones by identifying your limiting beliefs and changing them. How can you expect others to believe in you if you don't believe in yourself? Give those who have harmed you in the past your forgiveness. This includes individuals who have betrayed you, claimed credit for your accomplishments, and harmed you. Don't become obsessed with acquiring a specific position, fame, fortune, or material goods. These are ephemeral and will eventually vanish when you pass away. Instead, concentrate on developing and fully experiencing life. Relationships that don't benefit you should be ended. That includes unfavourable characters, liars, disrespectful individuals, harsh critics, and connections that limit your capacity for development. Spend time with those you get along with, including those who share your interests and who are upbeat, successful, and supportive of your advancement.

*"Moral authority comes from following universal and timeless principles like honesty, integrity, treating people with respect." -Stephen Covey*

"We spend money we don't have on goods we don't need in an effort to impress unconcerned individuals," William Smith observed. Nobody is impressed by your wealth, stylish attire, or taste in house furnishings. It must be so incredibly tiring to wear all these masks depending on your circumstances at any one time. Why do you think it's necessary for you to put on such a show? Don't let anyone convince you otherwise; you are wonderful just the way you are. Without a shred of guilt, share your original ideas, opinions, peculiarities, and personality traits with the world. Before making a choice, educate yourself and weigh your alternatives, but avoid being mired in uncertainty forever.

*"In the worst of times the best among us never lose their moral compass, and that is how they emerge relatively unscathed." - Henry Rollins*

Acquire the ability to see each occurrence impartially. So that you can apply the lessons going forward, concentrate on what you can learn from them. Arm yourself with as much knowledge as possible. Learn new things, take up new hobbies, and pursue new subjects of study. Develop a vast breadth of information for yourself. In video games, you can typically only level up to level 99, but in real life, you can level up indefinitely. What would you typically avoid doing? You become aware of who you are and what is significant in your life as you learn to embrace who you are. Perhaps most significantly, you begin to embrace life and truly love being alive.

*"Keep your thoughts positive because your thoughts become your words. Keep your words positive because your words become your behavior. Keep your behavior positive because your behavior becomes your habits. Keep your habits positive because your habits become your values. Keep your values positive because your values become your destiny."-Mahatma Gandhi*

## Change your perspective and Find happiness in the little things.

What if I told you that one of the most effective habits you can form to promote constant happiness is to cultivate grindfulness. Most likely, you'd ask, "What the heck is that?" Well, it is potent as is. Gratitude and mindfulness are combined in grindfulness. I'll elaborate. It's a good idea to practise thankfulness, but research reveals that we often limit what is deserving of our thanks and that our feelings of gratitude are often overwhelmed by life's annoyances and disappointments. For instance, you could be glad when your spouse books a weekend vacation for you and your closest friend, but you might not think to be grateful for the tiny things they do for you each day. Being aware is also very beneficial. Although it's more of a passive activity, mindfulness is being conscious of monitoring your thoughts and sensations and then calmly recognising them without judgement. It doesn't proactively encourage happiness. Gritfulness sits in the space between thankfulness and mindfulness. recognising and paying attention to the little things that make up the daily grind of life, and then expressing in the moment our gratitude and excitement for those little things. Consider a scenario in which you are travelling to the grocery store—a weekly chore you detest and are, to put it mildly, not in the mood for.

However, as you travel along, you notice how the leaves on the trees that line the road sparkle in the sunshine. So you stop to marvel at it in your head. Perhaps you're doing what you do every day and sending your first of several business emails for the day. Only this time, as you push send, you realise how quickly the email vanishes. You take a moment to wonder at how your words may travel thousands of kilometres via the radio and end up in someone else's mailbox. How is such technology even feasible, it's amazing. Grindfulness. It involves seeing and valuing small nuances during the monotonous daily routine. The slightest wonders influenced the mundane. It lowers the bar for things to be thankful for and conscious of, increases the frequency of expressing gratitude and thinking positively in the present, and, I guarantee you, it's a strong habit for positivity, you can build.

*If you follow your passion, you can build a life you're proud of.*

In his lifetime, Steve Jobs made a lot of progress. When he made those remarks, he argued, "Why else would we be here?" Unless not to act, alter, or accomplish something? To put it another way, our goal is to make a dent in the universe. Indeed, Steve Jobs left his imprint. Even after he has passed away, we still discuss him. Pharaoh Khufu also did so. He left us the great pyramid, though I don't like to credit individuals for a project's success when it's obvious that a group of people worked on it.

*"Carve your name on hearts, not tombstones. A legacy is etched into the minds of others and the stories they share about you."-Shannon Adler*

You are unlikely to experience true success or happiness if you believe, as do many people today, that happiness must wait while you succeed and that the ultimate goal of achievement is to abandon all efforts and live a happy life. A hot fudge sundae tastes great on the first bite, but after four, the pleasure is diminished, according to all scientific study on happiness. Instead than searching for some kind of eternal state of bliss, you need to refresh happiness on a regular basis.

*"We must believe that we are gifted for something and that this thing must be attained. Nothing in life is to be feared; it is only to be understood. I am one of those who thinks, like Nobel, that humanity will draw more good than evil from new discoveries. "-Marie Curie*

For a variety of reasons, having the appropriate mentality is crucial. Not least of all, in your situation, telling yourself that you couldn't do it because you felt so far outside of your comfort zone went against coaching theory and your own principles. You were really conflicted, and this is when your ego, posing as your impostor, sprung into action. Recall what a legacy is and that others who are ready and will benefit from it will see, cherish, and share it. Even if it can sound a little pompous to think about leaving a legacy, we all leave legacies as we live our lives. From the reflection that follows a discussion to the larger legacy a loved one leaves when they pass away to the legacy we leave when we part ways with a customer, team, or job.

*"Measuring life by one yardstick won't work. And moving through the four sequentially is a mistake too."-*
*Warren Buffett*

Life is a precious commodity. But how can you maximise your life? Here are some insightful suggestions from readers on how to maximise your time on earth.

- Being present and in the moment is the first step. I really enjoy the little things in life, such as the way flannel blankets feel against your skin, the warmth of a hug, or the gift of a smile. and appreciation.
- Create a magnificently chaotic patchwork of what is real for you and your position in our earthly community by taking all of your activities, beliefs, work, ideas, feelings, and contributions. With laughter and contemplation, they sew the patchwork together.
- Decorate courageously and with love. Recognize that patches occasionally wear out or rip, forcing you to determine whether you can repair them or whether you need to replace them. Pursue your hobbies and dreams right now!
- Never stop learning; develop the capacity for unconditional love and a passion for empirical learning.
- Live each day as though it were your last. Take risks and chances so that when you look back on your life, you can say you lived it to the fullest.

- Look after your body. Every element of your life is impacted by your level of health and fitness. Create and implement a time management strategy.
- Being open to and picky about ideas is one way to maximise your life. More concepts will be encountered, entertained, and pursued as though they were lovely to experience as our language is expanded.
- Stay in the present and show yourself and others love, kindness, and compassion.Evaluate your skills and talents realistically, then search for possibilities to use them in ways that advance human society in the future.
- "Push yourself on occasion." You could have more options than you think. When in doubt, use that other great human strength: the option that shows the most compassion.
- Take care of the ill, injured, and handicapped. Love, love, love, and when you think you have no more to give, love some more! Use your special abilities, knowledge, and insights to benefit others.
- The secret is to identify what makes you happy and useful. Speak up on behalf of those who can't. Make a difference in the life of someone else.
- Take care of your physical and mental health. Help others. and love unconditionally. Be concerned about the well-being of your family.
- Heal yourself if you need to, forgive others if you need to, and learn to love if that is your lesson. To get to the essence of existence, strive for a better, more meaningful life.
- As the answers to who you are and what you are destined to accomplish are personal to each of us, listen, breathe, and look for them. To act despite fear and to acknowledge and accept suffering and hurt.

- Accept and live as our authentic selves. Rely on your own sense of self to view people objectively, to perceive them clearly, and with compassion.
- Remain in the present and be certain that we are where we should be. Discover the fundamental nature of the mind by realising that thoughts and emotions are only fleeting clouds in the sky.
- Give someone helpful guidance or wisdom to assist them on their journey. It may significantly alter things. Try to be as present as possible at all times. Stop being so hard on yourself.
- Identify your importance to mankind and the existence of the planet on which we live. Show more consideration, kindness, and gentleness to our planet.We owe it to the environment, the wildlife, our forests, and our seas to bring them back to their former state of health.
- Assemble the things and people that bring you joy. Discover the advantages of knowing and accepting people from all walks of life. Follow your dreams, love the people you care about, and cultivate your spirit.
- Taking in life. Just do it. Don't live an unloved life. Constantly strive to put others' needs ahead of your own. Good karma may be created by doing something as simple as opening a door for someone else, allowing someone to go ahead of you in a line, or saying good morning to someone who is alone. "Volunteer your time."
- Always strive for love, both giving and receiving it. If you can look back on your life and say that you helped someone else feel loved, then your life was successful.
- Through your actions, words, music, and those you surround yourself with, you may cultivate a calm

environment. These are stimulating and can result in fantastic experiences. The mindful abilities of attention, compassion, and acceptance may assist you in transforming unhealthful behaviours into a way of being that symbolises freedom and inner peace.

- Remember to enjoy yourself. Work as hard as you can, and then watch a movie. When you're feeling perplexed, gaze up at the sky and take in how expansive everything is.

- Make plans and set goals, but be adaptable and resilient if they don't pan out. Peace can exist without you having to free yourself from negative ideas. Instead, turn your attention away from them and onto concepts that will enrich your life.

- Create sincere, real relationships with everyone you come into contact with, including your friends, family, coworkers, business partners, customers, clients, and acquaintances. Spend some time getting to know them better to build a deeper relationship.

- We are given opportunities to practise every day. We give our craft life when we practise it every day as a way of life rather than just a job. It might be a combination of physical, mental, and spiritual exercises.

- You'll know you've started a chain of goodwill because one act of kindness almost always leads to another, which should give you comfort even on the worst of days.

- Recognise what you've learnt from your mistakes, acknowledge that you can't undo the past, and begin to be nicer to yourself. The primary victim of holding a grudge against someone is you.

- The advantages of meditation for the mind-body connection are covered in prior works of mine. Many people think that in order to experience the benefits of this practise, they must spend hours in a contemplative position. We can choose. We may become mired in misery and disgust with our appearance. Alternately, we might accept who we are and disregard what people say about us.

- As we age, our learning frequently becomes stagnant. However, it's in our nature to always seek out new knowledge and information because otherwise we become bored. Therefore, invest in a book on a subject you are interested in. Enroll in an evening course or a course online.Expanding your knowledge will make you feel amazing, whether it's all theoretical or you're learning something useful.

*"Take up one idea. Make that one idea your life; dream of it; think of it; live on that idea. Let the brain, the body, muscles, nerves, every part of your body be full of that idea, and just leave every other idea alone. This is the way to success, and this is the way great spiritual giants are produced."- Swami Vivekanand*

The most significant sources of enjoyment in your life will be your connections with close relatives and friends. But you need to exercise caution. You will be persuaded to believe that you may put your investments in these relationships on hold when things at home appear to be going well. That would be a grave error. When severe issues in those relationships occur, it's frequently too late to fix them. This means that, almost paradoxically, it is most crucial to invest in creating strong families and personal friendships during times when it would seem unnecessary on the surface.

**"There is no strength where there is no battle."-Oprah Winfrey**

When all we experience in life are rainbows, adorable puppies, sugar drops, and sunlight, we have little reason to strive for personal improvement. Don't worry about what others are doing.

*A crucial component in the quest for success is overlooked when people get wrapped up in the manual that other people use. It does not always follow that something will work for you just because it did for someone else. Every fibre of your being should believe that you are capable of achieving everything you set your mind to.*

# CHAPTER TWO

# Changing Perspective And Improve Your Personal Productivity

*"You were born to win, but to be a winner, you must plan to win, prepare to win, and expect to win." --Zig Ziglar*

*You were born with exceptional talents and abilities.*

Many individuals underrate their potential and what they are capable of. The gap between where we are now and our potential is what we call potential. Potential frequently results in success for that person. This is not always about success (although for many, this is exactly what it is). Finding tranquilly is important to some people. Some people place more value on "being" than on "having" or "doing." Others care more about relationships and having the freedom to be themselves in order to meet the appropriate partner. Some claim that if we need to "unleash your potential," it suggests that something is wrong with us or that we are insufficient just as we are.

*"Life is full of beauty. Notice it. Notice the bumble bee, the small child, and the smiling faces. Smell the rain, and feel the wind. Live your life to the fullest potential, and fight for your dreams."-Ashley Smith*

Unleashing Potential, in my opinion, is about helping individuals realise their ambitions and aspirations, no matter what they may be, starting from where they are right now. It involves freeing individuals from the things that are preventing them from leading the life they desire and assisting in putting them in a position to succeed, whatever that may entail for them. You are incredibly capable and have all it takes to live the life of your dreams.

*"God, our Creator, has stored within our minds and personalities, great potential strength and ability. Prayer helps us tap and develop these powers."-A. P. J. Abdul Kalam*

Whether you are aware of it or not, you were born with exceptional talents and abilities. The narrative of your life is how you use it for your benefit and the benefit of others. Will this story help you realise your potential? Let's see if you can get things going! You are the only person in the world who truly understands how you feel. Let's face it. Others may make assumptions, conjectures, or inquiries, but they can never be certain.

*"Never underestimate the power of dreams and the influence of the human spirit. We are all the same in this notion: The potential for greatness lives within each of us."-Wilma Rudolph*

Abraham Maslow, a psychologist, used the term "actualization" to describe reaching our highest potential and being everything we may be. The effect is the second element. As we grow older, we must give the world the finest versions of ourselves in order to positively influence others and impact their lives. It's important because, for the majority of us, our purpose eventually has to be connected to something greater than ourselves. An example of a higher reason may be our family's or friends' happiness, a greater goal to change society in some way, or our religious adherence to a transcendent deity.

*"There will always be obstacles and challenges that stand in your way. Building mental strength will help you develop resilience to those potential hazards so you can continue on your journey to success."- Amy Morin*

The power you possess is something you yourself are unaware of. You may use your strength to get what you deserve in life by focusing all of your energy in the appropriate directions. You must use the power inside you to do it. Most of the time, you concentrate on difficulties rather than what may go well. You should perform a few rituals in order to focus your energies in the direction of your dreams. You may employ your entire potential and become alive by engaging in these rituals. We underrate our capacity to do more in life.

*"Too often we underestimate the power of a touch, a smile, a kind word, a listening ear, an honest compliment, or the smallest act of caring, all of which have the potential to turn a life around."- Leo Buscaglia*

We don't reach our full potential. Once you start using your power, you'll notice that your life is shifting toward far better and more fulfilling experiences. Your world is shaped by your thoughts. Your life is governed in part by your ideas. Take care of your thoughts. Our minds are quite strong. It complies with the directives we give it. That guidance is nothing more than our ideas. It will never operate at its best if we feed it doubt. Don't let small-minded and pessimistic thoughts limit your possibilities.

Your beliefs are formed by your ideas.

*"In life, it is important to not be afraid to put yourself out there, win or lose. It is all about the spirit of challenging yourself to be open to realizing your highest potential."- Cynthia Bailey*

A wonderful method to drive activity is by setting goals. It gives your following steps direction and helps to clear your mind. Goals that are challenging encourage the flow state that so many people want. Some people like to remark that "a life without challenge and danger is not worth living." Setting engaging, difficult, yet manageable goals is the secret to unlocking potential. The objective may be written down and spoken aloud. You need an alternative aim if it didn't inspire or move you, if you weren't motivated to act or weren't sure what to do. As Lao-Tzu once stated, "A journey of a thousand miles begins with a single step." To fully realise your potential, this is also true. Quickly assess your talents and limitations, identify the world's hunger you can alleviate, and establish ambitious goals for yourself. Then, use each day to take one tiny step in the right direction.

*"God puts people in our lives on purpose so we can help them succeed and help them become all He created them to be. Most people will not reach their full potential without somebody else believing in them."- Joel Osteen*

We make millions of decisions every day, most of them unconsciously. Your life is the total of all these choices, both small and large. For this reason, developing good behaviour is crucial. You could learn how to be grateful, manage stress, and have wholesome, motivating relationships. You might also discover how to change bad habits into good ones. Although they won't change overnight, once developed, they will have a favourable influence on hundreds of your judgments in the future.Resentment is one of the main causes of not reaching your full potential. "Resentment is like swallowing poison and waiting for the other person to die," Malachy McCourt once said.

- Do you intend to make significant changes in your life?
- Have you attempted to change but ended up reverting to your previous behaviour?
- Have you tried to form a habit but been unsuccessful?

Don't let other people influence your life to think negatively. Concentrate on the now since the past is over and the future is uncertain. Let the past not determine your future. Our sensitivity grows directly in proportion to how well we react to our impressions. Your awareness of the good things in your life will increase if you are grateful. You'll be more relaxed, you'll notice more opportunities, and your relationships will get better.

*"Everybody has a creative potential and from the moment you can express this creative potential, you can start changing the world."-Paulo Coelho*

Since this is the only life you have, I hope you fully realise all of your potential. I think you can do great things if you know what you have, understand how you can use it, let go of the painful past, and develop good habits over the daily steps you take. What would you do if you were not afraid? What if there were no boundaries that you had built for yourself in your life to unleash your potential ? What if your life's scrapes and bruises vanished, giving you the confidence to move forward?

## *What if you set down those bulky bags of useless items you're holding on to?*

Instead of being discouraged by the possibility of anything going wrong, what if you were inspired by what might be? Is it okay if you refuse to accept "I'll get by"?

- How would it feel to put your own pleasure ahead of your concerns about what other people think of you? What if you began to look forward to the journey rather than rushing to the end point just to be disappointed?
- If you had the opportunity to create the screenplay for this thing we call life, how would you do it?
- What if the love you long for was always present inside of you but you were too busy or frightened to feel it?
- What if the greatest danger of all is actually that you don't live the life you want to live?

*"Continuous effort, not strength or intelligence is the key to unlocking our potential."-Winston Churchill*

Your life is shaped by your beliefs. God has given each of us a special gift that is vast. However, we somehow fail to put it to use, and we go through life with false notions and unpleasant emotions. But you can always alter your thought process. Switch your negative ideas with optimistic ones. It works miracles. To reach your maximum potential, you must alter your ideas.

*We attempt to improve the outside world when we are in distress. But the truth is that we should pay attention to our inner selves and ideas.*

We have no control over the events or circumstances, but we do have power over our thoughts. Your beliefs are formed by your ideas. Your ideas are everything that makes up your beliefs. And your life is governed by your beliefs, whether they are false or true. The definition of believe, according to the dictionary, is an acceptance that something exists or is true, particularly one without proof.

*"Impossible is just a word thrown around by small men who find it easier to live in the world they've been given than to explore the power they have to change it. Impossible is not a fact. It's an opinion. Impossible is potential. Impossible is temporary. Impossible is nothing."*
*– Muhammad Ali*

Your life is hampered by these ideas. One must strengthen his mind if he wants to succeed. Never let your mind wander to unpleasant ideas. The first step you should take if you want to live the life of your dreams and achieve your objectives is to change your mindset from one of negativity and mediocrity to one of optimism and greatness. Your ideas have the potential to affect not only you but also other people. Because life is so brief, there's no use in doing something you'll later regret.

*"You measure the size of the accomplishment by the obstacles you have to overcome to reach your goals." -*
*Booker T. Washington*

You work at your highest capacity when you are doing what you love. This ultimately results in success and a happy life. There isn't a unique recipe for this. Those who are aware of this enjoy happy lives. Do you only get a job to get a paycheck? Are we only here to work, pay our bills, and pass away? Is that right? NoWe're all here to have happy lives. We are here to pursue our passions. Everything will come into your life naturally when you are doing what you love.

You'll be prosperous, wealthy, and well-known. Our mental and emotional health improves when we are engaged in what we enjoy. Your time and life are not worth living to please others. You are here to gratify yourself, not other people. Do what you love.

*"Some failure in life is inevitable. It is impossible to live without failing at something, unless you live so cautiously that you might as well not have lived at all -- in which case, you fail by default." - J.K. Rowling*

What occurs if your mother prepares the food you adore? Without her extending an invitation to join her at the table, you quickly grab it. You smell it first, then you see how it looks. As you begin to eat, use all of your senses. Your true strength comes from doing what you enjoy without regard for what others may think of you.

*Never give up. Today is hard, tomorrow will be worse, but the day after tomorrow will be sunshine.*

Change is a necessary part of life in order to fully realise our potential. "You simply have to accept things as they are and take no action." Given that our whole focus is on creating it, it is most likely the greatest discipline in the world. The key is to be present and trust the process. In the same vein, concentrate on what matters and let the rest go away. You don't have to take on more than is necessary at the moment. In actuality, doing less frequently produces better outcomes. A recycled thinking awareness is expressed through popular culture. If you want to fit in, there is a place for you, and you don't have to struggle to get there.

*"You don't learn to walk by following the rules. You learn by doing, and falling over." - Richard Branson*

Go out on a limb where the fruit is more rewarding if you want to be a thinker, a rebel, an innovator, an optimist, or a creative person, though. The world urges you to take chances. While some approaches encourage you to experience yourself with increased zest, those risks may or may not pay off. When we honour our actual nature rather than engaging in an internal conflict that we will ultimately lose, we can achieve the state of mind . Our determination to calm the turbulent thoughts in our heads so that the stillness can resonate throughout us leads to an effortless life. Lao Tzu tells us that when we synchronise with life's flow, everything—not just certain things, but all things, including the life we aspire to live—succeeds.

*"The people who are crazy enough to think they can change the world are the ones who do." - Steve Jobs*

We must begin acting in ways we haven't necessarily done previously if we want to gain confidence, and some of those ways will unavoidably be uncomfortable. People discuss what is comfortable and what is uncomfortable in conventional coaching and psychology. They'll say things like, "Everything you already have and do is inside your comfort zone, and everything you want is outside of it." They are not incorrect, but they are oversimplifying the situation and omitting a critical component. It sounds as though any place outside of your comfort zone will be uncomfortable when you say you only have to step outside of it to acquire what you want. But isn't that not the case? There is a slight distinction between viewing a snake safely contained in a glass tank via a pet store window and falling into a snake pit if you wish to overcome your fear of snakes.

Constantly comparing oneself to others is one of the most prevalent ways people lose their confidence without even recognising it. And since you're enrolled in this course, which implies that you must be educated and tolerant, I'm willing to wager that you even have a tendency to do that. However, you're generally only comparing yourself to individuals you perceive as the greatest or most outstanding people in your immediate environment.

*"A person should set his goals as early as he can and devote all his energy and talent to getting there. With enough effort, he may achieve it. Or he may find something that is even more rewarding. But in the end, no matter what the outcome, he will know he has been alive." - Walt Disney*

The ones who, in your subconscious, you believe are somehow superior to or more successful than you in some way. You then judge yourself because you aren't as good at it as they are because you compare yourself to what they do that you think they are so amazing at.

*"The future rewards those who press on. I don't have time to feel sorry for myself. I don't have time to complain. I'm going to press on." - Barack Obama*

However, if you were as good at it as they are, you wouldn't be comparing yourself to them but rather to someone who is even more skilled than they are. Nearly everyone engages in this. The real kicker is here. Most of the time, we also greatly underrate the people to whom we are making these comparisons. We only see what they want us to see, and whatever we see is impacted by our preconceived notions of them, which are frequently incorrect.

There is no quick route to success; only steadfast labour may make one's life's goals and aspirations a reality. We frequently hear people's justifications for giving up. "It wasn't meant to be," "It wasn't enjoyable anymore," or "Life is all about having fun" are typical lines of speech that are used in response. It's important to note that our minds are capable of creating whatever mental state we give them. Instead, we should impose a commitment state that will enable everyone to realise their own goals.

*A person who has expertise in a certain sector is more likely than others who lack experience to accomplish their life's goals and can operate shrewdly and effortlessly.*

This is still, without a doubt, the most difficult part of achieving successful objectives. What drives some people to relentlessly pursue their dreams while other people give up when things become tough? We get experience via hard labour, which enables us to learn a lot of new things. We may use this experience to develop clever thinking skills to successfully address a challenging issue. A person's ability to solve problems is enhanced through experience.

*"People who succeed have momentum. The more they succeed, the more they want to succeed, and the more they find a way to succeed. Similarly, when someone is failing, the tendency is to get on a downward spiral that can even become a self-fulfilling prophecy."- Tony Robbins*

Man needs his difficulties because they are necessary to enjoy success. Climbing to the top demands strength, whether it is to the top of Mount Everest or to the top of your career. Great dreams of great dreamers are always transcended.

A million people can smile because of MS Dhoni. He has been doing it since the early 2000s, when he first became one of Indian cricket's most recognisable figures. Dhoni has become one of the most admired cricket players in the world thanks to several notable on-field accomplishments. The captain of the Chennai Super Kings, who has left the international stage, never ceases to win over his admirers. Dhoni is adored by the public for more reasons than just the fact that he is the most successful captain India has ever produced. However, due to his attitude on the job, as a result, he is known as "Captain Cool."

I occasionally ponder how someone can maintain their composure in the face of so much pressure and expectation. You must be honest with yourself and with others. In life, you must be realistic and willing to take chances. However, you also need to be pragmatic. We all want to replicate Dhoni's calm demeanour, which has made him popular. Even in the most challenging games, we could always count on him to smile. His cool demeanour earned him the position of team captain. He had become his captain, in addition to realising his goal of playing with his hero Sachin. He helped the side to a resounding win in the ICC T-20 World Cup in 2007. He never stops inspiring the next generation with his outstanding leadership and original thoughts. Bollywood paid its respect to his brilliance with the film "Dhoni: The Untold Story."There are a lot of Inspirational qualities of MS Dhoni which makes him an idol for many youths.

*"I believe in giving 100%on the field and I don't really worry about the result if there's a great commitment on the field. That's a victory for me."-MS Dhoni*

MSD had seen a dream that many people dreaded seeing. Dhoni, who is from the little village of Ranchi, dared to dream and used bravery and guts to make that goal come true. From an early age, he looked up to cricket legend

Sachin Tendulkar and Bollywood star Amitabh Bachchan. He began his work with the Indian Railways as a ticket collector. He ultimately made it to international cricket in 2003 because of his dedication and never-say-die attitude. Dhoni, though, had a loftier aspiration, one that made him the greatest cricket skipper to represent India.

## *Aim for the stars, and you might just hit the moon, as the saying goes.*

Dhoni was known as an aggressive batter from a young age, but he didn't allow his ego to get in the way of picking up tips from other players. He picked up the helicopter shot from his pal, which eventually turned into one of Captain Cool's signature poses. In his school, Dhoni was the talk of the cricket team, and everyone used to admire him. Everyone around him was sad when he was rejected from the U-19 squad, but Dhoni made the decision to have a celebration. He put forth more effort to achieve where he is now because he valued the reality check provided by the snub. Dhoni used to finish his three-hour exam in only two and a half hours so he could head out and practise with his club. He balanced his love with his academics. He continued to attend practises even after starting a full-time job and working long hours every day at the train station. Dhoni held a regular government position. His family was content, and he might have led a prosperous life as well. Instead, he made a huge leap.

*The sensation of zeal you have from someone or something that provides you with fresh, imaginative things to accomplish is referred to as inspiration.*

When we are young, we create goals and aspirations that we want to achieve. In order to do that, we need to have the necessary information, abilities, and, most importantly, confidence to make all of these things stronger. For the same reason, we make an effort to follow anybody who can provide us with the support we need to accomplish all or any of these things, as doing so motivates us to pursue our aspirations. You get self-assurance that you can achieve something when you see that person or hear their remarks. Our parents are the first people who inspire us all because they help us develop the confidence we need to begin thinking rationally.

Over the past five years, this has been my area of interest. After observing human behaviour, I came to the conclusion that success is only possible for successful people because they have an insatiable appetite for achievement. When you have a burning desire to succeed, obstacles and setbacks become nothing more than speed bumps.

*Roadblocks and failures become speed bumps in your way when you have an unquenchable appetite combined with dedication and effort to accomplish a goal.*

You will get various experiences via hard labour, which will strengthen and improve you as a person. Simply be patient and believe in yourself. We want to be respected by those around us and have our thoughts valued. This is exactly what hard work and self-esteem boosting bring us. People always value those that put in the effort and are aware of their potential, regardless of how successful they are currently or will be. Working hard will help you improve every day and every moment. We frequently reflect on our past and ask ourselves, "What have we learned?" Working hard makes us better in every way; it turns a novice into an expert. Growth is not possible without effort.

*"You can't connect the dots looking forward; you can only connect them looking backwards." So you have to trust that the dots will somehow connect in your future. You have to trust in something—your gut, destiny, life, karma, whatever. This approach has never let me down, and it has made all the difference in my life. " -Steve Jobs*

No matter what your career, you must take challenges and come out of your comfort zone, and your humble background can't be an excuse if you fail. It is quite challenging to succeed in life if you don't respect others, whether they are your own or anybody else's. Let's imagine that when you enter any large building, you must treat everyone equally, from the first man you encounter to the managing director, for example. Go through the challenging time; struggle through it, but if you can do it with a grin, I am giving those great examples of people, perhaps five people, who set examples through their lives and can truly pull it off. Because we sometimes complain about life and the difficult times, it's vital to remember that it's going through the difficult moments that will really help you become a better person. I hope it is the start of something amazing and mind-blowing for you.

*Every challenge you encounter has a single underlying question: how do you deal with yourself? An inability to manage what I refer to as the "You-Factor" is at the root of all of your stumbles, errors, and failures. &; The You-Factor is about managing yourself and your entire life properly, more so than self-worth or self-respect, even beyond character and sense of purpose.*

I will illustrate how your thoughts may impact your mental, emotional, social, and physical health. It also covers the subject of how your willpower and visions might help you achieve inner tranquilly. A step-by-step examination of overcoming the internal obstacles to achievement may be found in from passion to peace. You must restrict or eradicate unproductive behaviours while imposing new habits that boost productivity if you want to have the desire and motivation required to consistently put out the level of effort required for productivity.

*"Often we don't even realise who we're meant to be because we're so busy trying to live out someone else's ideas. But other people and their opinions hold no power in defining our destiny."- Oprah Winfrey*

Oprah Winfrey's inspiring but painful success story Oprah had a difficult upbringing, growing up in poverty as the child of a single, underage mother. Because of the sexual assault she endured as a youngster, she had a difficult, rebellious adolescence. When she was thirteen, she fled her home. Oprah, despite having a challenging background, refused to let the past dictate her future. She served as proof that no matter what challenges we encounter, with passion, perseverance, and hard work, we can do anything.

*"Passion is energy. Feel the power that comes from focusing on what excites you" – Oprah Winfrey*

She had a variety of odd occupations as a child before getting a job as the local news anchor at a tiny radio network. She later began her own chat show while working for a TV station. She became a fan favourite thanks to her moving performance in that programme. Her television programme thus became one of the most popular programmes ever. Oprah had a lot of hardship as a child as a result of poverty. So, as she rose to fame, she gave money to the poor in an effort to make the world a better place to live. She is regarded as one of the greatest philanthropists of colour and one of the most powerful people in the world today. She has a $3 billion net worth, placing her among the all-time most prosperous businesswomen. Oprah has been dubbed the most influential woman of her generation by Life magazine. According to Business Week, she is the biggest African American philanthropist in American history.

## How can you change your view to have a positive outlook?

If you alter your perspective, the difficulties of life might become more bearable. You may adopt a more upbeat view by using these suggestions for perspective switching.

- Sing aloud an uplifting inner monologue. Make a conscious effort to employ the power of positivity to actively alter your inner dialogue because it's common for self-talk to be negative in nature. Set a daily reminder to think happy thoughts to boost your confidence and make you feel better. Even better, each morning, compose and repeat a longer affirmation.

- Help others by volunteering. Helping others and performing small acts of kindness may greatly improve your outlook. You can not only put your life in perspective, but it may also divert your attention from your troubles and generally uplift your mood.

- Think about helping out in a hospital or soup kitchen. Your life will become more meaningful if you acknowledge that you are healthy and have the resources to sustain yourself. By doing this, you may also actively decide to alter the negative aspects of your life.

- You may alter your viewpoint by helping friends and family members since you are making them feel good, which in turn makes you feel good.

- Take into account fresh data and other people's viewpoints. Ensure that you take into account the knowledge you've gained via school, experience, and speaking with others as you start to create your new viewpoint. Without this essential knowledge, you won't be able to grow or alter your viewpoints. As you take this new knowledge into account, keep the overall picture in mind and concentrate on forming well-rounded opinions.

- Recognise that you don't have to agree with everyone's viewpoints. Based on what you've discovered throughout your investigation, you can pick and choose which of their viewpoints you like. Describe and put into action your new viewpoint. You're now prepared to completely express your altered perspective and put it into practise in your daily life. This will not only support your own new viewpoint but also let others know that you have changed.

- To bring about a beneficial transformation in your life, put fresh perspectives into practise. So that you have a concrete recollection of your new perspectives, write them down on a sheet of paper. You can put your new perspectives into action in a variety of ways, from holding discussions to making a difference in the world.

*Your outlook on life will become more optimistic as you give and receive love and support.*

How often have you heard that success comes from hard work? Undoubtedly a great deal, and it's true! Success is mostly dependent on effort, and this is true for many different reasons. Let's first discuss why working hard matters before we go into our arguments for why it's essential for success. Working hard enables you to gradually improve your level of self-discipline. Even though procrastination may make even the simplest chores more difficult to complete, we occasionally nevertheless self-destruct. Sometimes we don't even know why we do it! But if you are committed to working hard, self-control will come. This is another another example of why perseverance is essential for success.

*Working towards your goals and dreams can be challenging because the path to success is always a bumpy one.*

Because people like to reward those who are willing to put up the effort necessary to complete all duties in order to succeed in life, hard work is something that has to be recognised. A person with discipline, devotion, and resolve to succeed in life is someone who works hard enough. You can achieve anything with effort. We have heard this piece of advice so frequently that its original meaning has been obscured. The issue is that despite our seeming laborious efforts, nothing seems to be happening. Many worthwhile goals in life need a lot of hard work to be accomplished. It's possible that working hard isn't always enjoyable or desirable. When you put off a difficult job, issues may develop in a variety of ways later. Laziness, which has a variety of negative effects on our lives, can be encouraged by avoiding hard labour.

*"Success does not mean an absence of problems, it is overcoming problems. Success is not measured by how high we go up in life, but how many times we bounce back when we fall down." — Shiv Khera*

In today's world, successful individuals are easy to come by. Every time we turn on the television, we see pictures of sportsmen being celebrated for their victories. We read articles in newspapers and publications about successful businesspeople scheming for their next lucrative investment idea. Our favourite actors and actresses may be found in movies as well, and they frequently amass more wealth through their labour in a single year than some of us will ever see. The media is prepared to show us the outcomes of these people, but they omit to reveal the processes involved. All of these folks put forth a lot of effort and commitment to get where they are. People compete for top honours and grades in school and college, for better positions at work, and to launch their own businesses in our world of continual competition. I will share the most inspiring stories of those who used their indomitable perseverence to accomplish their goals on this planet.

*"I've missed more than 9,000 shots in my career. I've lost almost 300 games. 26 times, I've been trusted to take the game winning shot and missed. I've failed over and over and over again in my life. And that is why I succeed."- Michael Jordan*

Any NBA fan, or anybody for that matter, will immediately mention one player when asked who the greatest basketball player of all time is. Basketball legend Michael Jordan is regarded by the association, the public, and even his fellow players. Michael, according to those who saw him grow up, was competitive in practically everything. He was a competitive person who actually hated losing. He thus took his exclusion from his high school's varsity squad quite personally. Most people agree that Michael Jordan is the best basketball player to ever play the game. He won four gold medals with USA Basketball, including two at the Olympics, and was twice recognised as the sport's top male athlete. He served as the NBA's spokesperson for more than ten years. He decided to change careers after that. How could a guy walk away from success when he was at the height of his power?

*"My attitude is that if you push me towards something that you think is a weakness, then I will turn that perceived weakness into a strength."- Michael Jordan*

There is a phenomenon in psychology known as the halo effect. The halo effect, put simply, is the propensity for individuals to confuse one favourable feature with another. As a result, when we meet someone who appears intelligent, for instance, we also often think that they are amusing, kind, or possess any other trait we place a high value on. And although it's not always true, we have a tendency to think that successful deals are synonymous with success.

Any individual who has achieved great success has failed, sometimes on a huge, humiliating scale. Stop being scared to put in the effort and fail, because no one who is successful will ever condemn you for it. Only those who have never failed themselves will ever condemn you, generally because they have made extremely safe decisions. Face your concerns, quit being frightened of failing, and go with the task at hand. Putting in the effort is how you develop bravery and start moving in the direction of being your best self.

*"Do the one thing you think you cannot do. Fail at it. Try again. Do better the second time. The only people who never tumble are those who never mount the high wire. This is your moment. Own it." - Oprah Winfrey*

You are sad because you are not realising your potential or attaining your ambitions. First of all, be aware that you are not alone; this occurs to everyone. You are capable of improving. It will take a lot of effort, bravery, and grit, but if you persevere and have faith in yourself, you will succeed in your endeavours and become the finest version of yourself. Instead of spending more time working on a project that requires attention, going to the gym, preparing supper at home, etc., it would be nice to unwind, watch a movie or a show, meet a friend for dinner, etc.

*"If you're not stubborn, you'll give up on experiments too soon. And if you're not flexible, you'll pound your head against the wall and you won't see a different solution to a problem you're trying to solve." - Jeff Bezos*

Therefore, when we seek out others to contrast ourselves with, we don't just tend to seek out those we believe to be superior to us in some way; rather, once we find one quality in them that we would rate higher than our own, the halo effect takes over and leads us to believe that they possess a multitude of qualities superior to our own, whether or not that is actually the case. And now is the time to begin executing both of those actions.

The best way to achieve it, though, is to choose the appropriate person to compare oneself to in the first place, as it is extremely difficult to manage cognitive biases like the halo effect.

In any case, there is only one person to whom we should be compared. And that is who we were before. Because the only way to determine whether your progress is being made is to compare where you are right now to where you wanted to be one week, one month, or one year ago.

It's excellent that you're closer; keep up the good effort. If you're not, you'll need to either start working or switch to a different type of employment that is more effective. In any case, there is only one person to whom we should be compared. And that is who we were before. Because the only way to determine whether your progress is being made is to compare where you are right now to where you wanted to be one week, one month, or one year ago. It's excellent that you're closer; keep up the good effort. If you're not, you'll need to either start working or switch to a different type of employment that is more effective.

*"The question I ask myself like almost every day is, 'Am I doing the most important thing I could be doing?'" - Mark Zuckerberg*

The best of the best, the top performers, act in this manner for three straightforward reasons. They don't worry about what other people are doing. They understand that their personal outcomes don't have to be influenced by those of others. And they are aware that continuing to develop from where they are now is the only way to enhance their outcomes.

You will experience an immediate and long-lasting boost in your confidence once you stop comparing yourself to other people and begin comparing yourself to your previous self while working on living in your growth zone, developing your super ego, and mastering the other techniques and philosophies from this course. Here is your straightforward workout. Every week, set aside a specific day and time to sit down and spend a few minutes comparing your present self to your past self. Note your current position in relation to where you were a month, six months, or a year ago.

- What steps have you taken to get closer to your objectives?
- What part of your life has changed?

The answers you discover should indicate what you need to do more of to get the desired results. The secret is to identify your strengths so you can capitalise on them. Frederick Buechner, a theologian, once observed that "your calling is where your passions meet the needs of the world."

*"I think goals should never be easy, they should force you to work, even if they are uncomfortable at the time." -*
*Michael Phelps*

It is a good idea to consider how you may use your skills and limitations to better the world if you are aware of them. Asking your friends and coworkers to name your five strengths and one flaw might be all that is required. The second important question you must ask yourself is, "How can I develop in these areas?"

*"You can only become truly accomplished at something you love. Don't make money your goal. Instead, pursue the things you love doing, and then do them so well that people can't take their eyes off you." - Maya Angelou*

People typically regret the things they did not do rather than the ones they did when they are facing death. There are many difficulties and anxieties in life, but you may ask yourself a few questions: When I'm older, would I regret not doing this? Will I still remember this in ten years? How important is it to me? If I don't do this, will I be able to look in the mirror? You must have courage to realise your potential; otherwise, you will end up going in circles.

I would begin any of these undertakings in the same way. However, following these procedures alone won't help; you also need mentors, in-depth knowledge, and practise time. The learning curve for one of these initiatives will be severe until you figure it out and can really make things happen. People often wait for a better chance, a better opportunity, or a better occasion in life—a future moment when the universe will align perfectly. When this day eventually arrives, you will feel prepared to take immediate action. However, the day won't come unless you decide that it will.

*"To live a fulfilled life, we need to keep creating the "what is next", of our lives. Without dreams and goals there is no living, only merely existing, and that is not why we are here." - Mark Twain*

You may overcome the difficulties in life by teaching yourself to think more positively. Although changing your viewpoint or perspective is not simple, these suggestions might serve as a useful road map.

Reframing your mental attitude toward commonplace events is a simple technique to gain a positive viewpoint in any aspect of your life. You may discover a silver lining by reminding yourself that you "get to" do something rather than telling yourself that you "had to" do it. Saying, "I have to clean the home," for instance, carries a negative connotation since it frames cleaning as an unwelcome obligation. On the other hand, saying, "I get to clean the home," reframes the work as something you look forward to, highlighting the importance of having a place to live in the first place. Reframing daily duties with a positive outlook is a terrific technique to shift your perspective and enhance your mental well-being.

Positivity may be aided by altering your viewpoint to concentrate on the broader picture. Thinking from a micro-perspective can be dangerous because a minor unpleasant incident can easily send your thoughts spiralling downward. It's simpler to stop worrying about the little things when you concentrate on the bigger picture.

Consider things from a new angle. Looking at the problem from a new perspective can frequently be useful when you're irritated by someone else's conduct. You might be able to sympathise with and comprehend the other person's actions if you try to see the issue from their perspective.

Eliminate all bad energy from your life. When you are surrounded by terrible objects or individuals who continually feed you negative thoughts, it is difficult to think positively. It could be better to minimise your time engaging in activities that make you feel down, such as surfing social media or reading the news, and instead focus on activities that make you feel good or are productive. Likewise, if a member of your family or a close friend consistently draws you into their orbit of bad energy, opt to spend your time with more upbeat individuals.

*An important first step in the pursuit of living your greatest life may be to surround yourself with optimism.*

Your view on yourself and life is influenced by the people you spend time with, including family and friends. Limiting oneself to particular individuals or groups of individuals may make it more difficult for you to alter your viewpoints. Your perceptions are significantly impacted by education and learning. Your opinions may not change if you don't keep up with current events.

Although shifting your attitude will involve a lot of work to better your own life, you'll also discover how good it feels to be able to assist others. Find a friend, family member, coworker, or stranger who is struggling, and do something kind to make their day better—even if it requires stepping outside of your comfort zone.

Imagine how different your life would be if you had a different viewpoint. Consider how your life might be different if you had different perspectives after reflecting on your own and what influences them. This can enable you to start shifting your thoughts as well as seeing their advantages.

Consider your perspectives and how they have influenced you. Consider your numerous viewpoints and how they affect the way you see the world and yourself. You may begin to make adjustments proactively by taking their viewpoints into account. Make a list of your viewpoints on paper to make them easier to notice and consider. On each section, you can add notes or comments as needed. It will be simpler to modify your perspectives if you are really honest with yourself about them.

Perhaps you'd like to be less tense or reactive, or maybe you'd like your life to be more balanced or fun. You could wish to act as a calming force for your family or team. Your why is significant, and genuinely realising and experiencing it can help you be more committed to using what you have learned. Speaking of applying your knowledge, you are now able to identify when you are in one of the three autonomic states and are familiar with some basic techniques for controlling your neural system. You are aware of your pressures and your resources for overcoming them. In light of that, I urge you to create a strategy that is unique to you by pledging to control your nervous system. I want you to make a few pledges about how you're going to react to stressors and when you find yourself caught in a mobilised or immobilised condition.

Let me give you a few illustrations of how these obligations could seem. When I spend the first half of morning on Zoom, I promise to get up and go for a little stroll after lunch. When I'm in Zoom meetings, I enjoy sipping on a cup of hot tea. I make a commitment to contacting this person who grounds me when I have a one-on-one engagement with a team member or customer that stresses me out. I make a commitment to listening to music as I work during the day when I'm stressed out about a deadline because it makes me feel more creative and less blocked. When you have your list, go through it aloud to yourself and ask yourself whether each commitment makes you feel secure and connected. If so, you've hit the mark. If any make you feel nervous or overwhelmed, or if you don't notice any sensation associated with it, rework your commitment until it appears to be the proper sise for you. By creating this list of commitments, you're committing to yourself on a deeper level that your why matters and that you're prepared to create a plan of action based on what you've learned.

## *There's always a way to do it better.*

Personal productivity is the effective completion of tasks that advance your goals while preserving equilibrium in significant spheres of your life. Depending on what's important to you, being more productive on a personal level may imply many things, such as fostering social connections, improving one's health, or boosting one's income. In the end, setting the proper priorities is the key to achieving your objectives while avoiding burnout.

**"Productivity is never an accident. It is always the result of a commitment to excellence, intelligent planning, and focused effort."**

Productivity is not only a trendy word. Personal productivity is the effectiveness with which you continuously execute things that are essential to you. The topic of productivity is frequently brought up in relation to the job. However, given the growing overlap between our personal and professional lives, we should value personal productivity equally.

## *Effective performance is preceded by painstaking preparation.*

When most individuals strive to be more productive, they concentrate on how to get more done in a day rather than considering if those things actually warrant taking up so much time and energy. Put your focus on what you can work on rather than setting a goal that you can compete in a single day. In actuality, little or no management activities are frequently those that may be finished in a single day.

That is to say, they are essential, but they won't significantly advance your life, and more importantly, they shouldn't serve as the yardstick by which you judge your productivity. Because they lack a broad, long-term vision for what their life should be, a lot of people become trapped attempting to complete an increasing number of those little, everyday activities.

*Sometimes, things may not go your way, but the effort should be there every single night.*

This occurs as a result of people trying to attain goals that are excessively particular rather than constructing their life goals based on values, emotions, and "big picture" elements. You must sit down and write out your ultimate vision for your life as the first and most crucial step towards changing your life and moving ahead.

**"People often remark that I'm pretty lucky. Luck is only important in so far as getting the chance to sell yourself at the right moment. After that, you've got to have talent and know how to use it." -Frank Sinatra**

Don't forget to think about how you want to feel, what you want to do every day, who you want to be with, and how you want to spend your time. Place a printed copy of it on the wall in front of your primary workspace. Frequently, what's actually not working in our lives isn't what's hurting us the most; rather, it's what makes us feel the least inspired and driven. Pain is a tough thing since it really plays a role in achieving most of our objectives. Not at all. What we're seeking to prevent is suffering and discomfort. However, lack of drive, indifference, and apathy are the clear symptoms that you aren't working on a project that actually interests you, and you should reconsider. Use your past blunders as a type of manual for what not to do rather than criticising where you are right now.

*"Believe in yourself! Have faith in your abilities! Without a humble but reasonable confidence in your own powers you cannot be successful or happy." --Norman Vincent Peale*

Being aware of your dissatisfaction with how a certain course of action affected you is highly important information to have. Appreciate that you were ready to take chances and try new things instead of viewing it as a moral failing or a sign of your lack of value or skill, and go on with even more wisdom about what you do and don't care about, as well as what works and doesn't for your life. One place of one's own is one of the fundamental requirements for humans to flourish. A workstation, a bedroom, a whole apartment, or a house can all qualify as this. The key is to claim some real estate and put some effort into making it a place you not only want to be but also somewhere that motivates you to become the person you really want to be. If your home is full of mementos from the past, ones that don't evoke happy recollections or encourage new ideas, you won't be able to move ahead. If your desk is messy and it bothers you, you won't be able to move forward.

If you don't actively make the effort to create an area where your work is expressly defined, you will never feel at ease anywhere. It's crucial, yet frequently disregarded. Remember that your frame of reference is limited to what you have experienced when you envision how your life will be in the coming year and beyond. You'll probably feel a little uneasy or frightened when you imagine something that is better than what you have previously experienced.

*"No matter how many personal productivity techniques you master, there will always be more to do than you can ever accomplish in the time you have available to you, no matter how much it is." --Brian Tracy*

A surprising level of dread is typically also accompanied by significant, broad change. Accept this as it comes. Be receptive to how your life may develop in ways that go beyond what you can now imagine. The reason why most individuals succumb to their worst tendencies isn't because they lack the desire to change their lives drastically; rather, it's that they don't realise that breakthroughs don't just happen on their own. They are an outcome of microshifts.

*"Efficiency is doing things right; effectiveness is doing the right things."-Peter Drucker*

Let's take the scenario where you wish to slim down. Your body will be shocked if you start changing your food and exercise programme too radically, and you'll rapidly return to your cosy homeostasis. Instead, begin with subtle, nearly imperceptible adjustments. Let's suppose you only eat one snack each day (let's suppose it has a total caloric value of 250). If everything else in your life remained the same, you would lose a pound every two weeks, or 26 pounds in a year. All from skipping a single snack. The purpose isn't to praise dieting methods (most "dieting" doesn't work, anyhow), but rather to emphasise how even seemingly insignificant behaviours may have a significant influence on your life and how altering these habits can affect major aspects of your life. It's often a lot easier than you think.

*"The really happy people are those who have broken the chains of procrastination, those who find satisfaction in doing the job at hand. They're full of eagerness, zest, productivity. You can be, too." -- Norman Vincent Peale*

If you try to design your life around what you believe will provide you with the most comfort, you will be constantly disappointed.The question is actually what you feel is worth the agony, since nothing in life is without its own unique set of difficulties. A productive year doesn't always imply you finished a lot of unimportant chores. It indicates that you have been intentional with your time and have made efforts to improve your future enjoyment of life. Consider this when you are working each day: Could I do this for the rest of my life? If not, why not? That will provide a wealth of information about what is and isn't actually effective. I completely agree with what Charles R. Swindoll once said, "If you are going to achieve excellence in big things, you develop the habit in little matters. Excellence is not an exception, it is a prevailing attitude."

Regardless of who you are or what stage of life you are in, organising your funds is essential. Working on lowering your monthly expenses, maintaining a low overhead, paying off debt, and increasing your emergency savings and investment capital will be critical for allowing you to take risks, stabilise your life, and reduce your financial anxiety. I'm sorry to have to break it to you, but scaling up in your company, lowering your weight by 10 pounds, and improving your profit margin won't make you happy. Such tangible progress is crucial. Not nothing, really. But it's not everything either. Instead of listening to your emotionally charged self-talk story about your life, connect to your reality and start living it.

*"The biggest risk is not taking any risk... In a world that changing really quickly, the only strategy that is guaranteed to fail is not taking risks."- Mark Zuckerberg, Facebook*

You may experience true joy every day by focusing on the present and all that you have to be thankful for in it. In order to accomplish this, you must ask yourself what is actually occurring as opposed to what is occurring in your internal narrative. Perhaps you've always struggled with money, so you think that one of your main objectives should be to increase your income. In actuality, you could be financially secure and prefer to focus on hobbies or personal interests outside of work. You must keep in mind that frequently, what we desire most is simply what we need.

*"Opportunity is missed by most people because it is dressed in overalls and looks like work."-Thomas Edison*

Above everything else, we look for familiarity and comfort. Perhaps posting often on social media and working to create a community around your product or service are requirements of your company plan. If so, set aside a day to plan and draught every article, then use a scheduling tool to schedule postings for the following week, month, or longer. Be careful to make it as simple and accessible as possible for yourself to do the things you care about and need to prioritise.

*"If you cannot do great things, do small things in a great way." -Napolean Hill*

If a coffee shop is where you produce your finest work, go there. Disable your push alerts if you need peace and quiet to concentrate. Make it simple for you to continue to meet your needs. Your energy, not your time, is limited on a daily basis. The major secret is that the direction that the majority of your energy is focused on directly affects your life. If you want to make significant changes, decide what matters most to you and what matters least to you, and then let those things go. If you are unable to locate someone to assist you, consider if you actually require it. Use your energy on something you truly care about if the response is a resounding nay.

*Life is short, live it. Love is rare, grab it. Anger is bad, dump it. Fear is awful, face it. Memories are sweet, cherish them.*

If you don't allow yourself to be happy and allow your life to be excellent right here and right now, you may work on your life for the next 12 months straight and, while making a lot of external progress, you won't feel very different on the inside. Nothing short of altering your daily thoughts and emotions will alter your outlook, perspective, or internal narrative that governs your thoughts and feelings. I'll start now. Not until you've made more progress. Not once you've changed or improved. In reality, altering your life only entails altering your current state of being. The rest will be handled automatically.

*"Plans are nothing; planning is everything." --Dwight D. Eisenhower*

Instant gratification is alluring and enjoyable, but it shouldn't come at the price of long-term objectives, particularly those that will help you improve your self-esteem and move you closer to your objectives. You will undoubtedly come across an explanation or justification if you are seeking one not to act morally. Unless you did anything to deserve a response, the likelihood is that when someone makes a comment, offers unsolicited advice, or treats you rudely, the statement says more about the person than it does about you.

*Walk away from anything or anyone who takes away from your joy. Life is too short to put up with fools.*

Change into some new clothing and go workout if you need to feel better right now. Endorphins make you joyful, relieve tension, and aid in mental clarity. Get some perspective by working out first, then returning to the subject. It's likely that after exercising, your emotions will be more stable, your intellect will be sharper, and your anxiety level will be lower than before.

**"There are risks and costs to action. But they are far less than the long-range risks of comfortable inaction."**
**--John F. Kennedy**

Therefore, try to see if you can get some exercise before you make a choice if you panic and feel overwhelmed by whatever you have been faced with. You'll come to a judgement that is less emotional and more based on logic than on emotion. Start attempting to track and modify these behaviours if you see that you spend a lot of time looking at multiple devices, frequently checking social media, or aimlessly using your phone. Whatever your primary source of ineffectiveness is, learn to control it so you can become more efficient and stop wasting time.

**"He who asks is a fool for five minutes, but he who does not ask remains a fool forever."-Anonymous**

You do have some influence over your life at any given time; you are not a victim of every whim and situation. Whether you can alter your circumstances depends on how you use that control. The sooner you stop avoiding taking responsibility for your life and stop blaming others, the more autonomy you will have, the sooner you will start doing the work, and the sooner you will start progressing.

***"I feel that luck is preparation meeting opportunity."-Oprah Winfrey***

Living your life selfishly for yourself will not bring you the most fulfilment. The times when we are choosing to contribute to others are when we experience the most happiness and fulfilment, on the other hand. Every day, give someone else your life. Encourage a young person. Support a coworker. Support a nearby nonprofit. Or simply give your friend who needs to hear from you a call. You have aspirations, objectives, and hopes in addition to the daily needs of existence.

***"Paying attention to the minor things rather than the big ones is the foundation of success in life."- Booker T. Washington***

You enjoy doing hobbies and participating in activities that define who you are. Take use of these possibilities to live. And each day, engage in one activity you enjoy. We all have tasks that we need to complete, including projects, jobs, and obligations. Most likely, you can't complete everything on your to-do list in a single day. But to get the most out of today, choose one major item off your list and complete it first. If you're done, go to the next one. Our days are made up primarily of single days that follow one another. The sun rises, sets, and rises once more. And ultimately, the lives we decide to lead will depend on the way we choose to live each day.

***"It is not enough to be busy, so are the ants. The question is: What are we busy about?" – Henry David Thoreau***

It won't be easy to increase your personal productivity, but every obstacle you overcome is a chance to get better. Since people have been trying to increase productivity ever since the dawn of time, it's not surprising that there are so many quotations on the subject. The fact that "productivity" applies to practically every facet of life doesn't help. You will learn to better manage your time, energy, and attention by learning from the distractions you encounter and the errors you make. The simple fact that you have a North Star will inspire you to keep moving forward despite all of the potential barriers.

*"Use your mind to think about things, rather than think of them. You want to be adding value as you think about projects and people, not simply reminding yourself they exist."- David Allen*

## *The beginning of life is beyond your comfort zone.*

Why are so many of us scared to leave our comfort zones, although it has long been believed that life begins at the other end? I'll tell you why: being in your comfort zone reduces worry and tension. This makes it quite simple to never cross the line since, let's face it, being in your own safety bubble is pretty darn comfortable.

*"Your work is going to fill a large part of your life, and the only way to be truly satisfied is to do what you believe is great work. And the only way to do great work is to love what you do. If you haven't found it yet, keep looking. Don't settle. As with all matters of the heart, you'll know when you find it." --Steve Jobs*

Some people find it impossible to imagine leaving their safety bubble, especially if you are confident that you will experience anxiety. Having said that, we all occasionally need a little more incentive to face our fears and leave the safety of our comfort zones.

*"As you move outside of your comfort zone, what was once the unknown and frightening becomes your new normal." -Robin S. Sharma*

Discover your comfort zone, then unwind for a while. Once you've changed your challenge to something more manageable and within your growth range, try it again. Now, when you're in your growth zone, you might occasionally experience some uneasy feelings, but they'll be a lot easier to handle. These emotions may include apprehension, mild anxiety, discomfort, stress, and even a small amount of fear. And that's totally okay. It's not your intention to never feel these emotions.

## *The comfort zone is nothing else but a graveyard for your dreams & ideas.*

Getting comfortable doing what you should or need to do in spite of them is your goal. To put it another way, you want to get used to being a little uncomfortable. The wonderful thing is that after some time spent in your growth zone, your subconscious mind, which was previously serving up all kinds of anxious, stressed-out, or apprehensive thinking, starts to recognise that you are completely safe. And when it does, it alters those beliefs and begins to give you thoughts about what you're doing that are relaxed, secure, confident, or even happy and excited.

Alter begins at the end of your comfort zone; you never change your life until you move out of your comfort zone. Instead of telling ourselves lies and making up reasons to stay in our comfort zones, we must be honest about what we want and take risks.

So, as you can see, this is not how the comfort zone is modelled. It extends beyond the inside and outside. In order to master the skill of leaving our comfort zone in healthy and beneficial ways, there are two additional zones that we should be aware of. Because some actions that are outside of our comfort zone—like falling into a pit of snakes—are so far from it, taking them will induce psychological distress.

*"You can choose courage or you can choose comfort. You cannot have both." -Brene Brown*

Additionally, after going through anything painful, we often try to avoid it in the future. These things fall into what we call the panic zone, and entering the panic zone can cause us to withdraw from an activity or a circumstance to the point where we give up on ever mastering it. What, therefore, should we do instead?

*"The hardest thing to do is leaving your comfort zone. But you have to let go of the life you're familiar with and take the risk to live the life you dream about." -T. Arigo*

Your comfort zone begins to enlarge as a result and catches up with you. And as a result, the activities you were doing outside of your comfort zone will now move inside of it. And everything changes when that occurs. As you can see, your comfort zone and your panic zone have a predetermined relationship. This implies that the panic zone is pushed farther out when your comfort zone grows to incorporate anything new.

*By leaving your comfort zone behind and taking a leap of faith into something new, you find out who you are truly capable of becoming.*

This allows you to start practising and mastering things that were previously in your panic zone and have them slide into your growth zone. And as you continue to do so, more and more items will inevitably migrate from your growth zone into your comfort zone, which will eventually include everything you want to feel secure and at ease about. That sounds good, doesn't it?

*"We have to be honest about what we want and take risks rather than lie to ourselves and make excuses to stay in our comfort zone." -Ray Bennett*

Making your own growth zone workouts is a fantastic way to build your confidence, acquire new knowledge, and increase your experience. And you may start doing that in whichever parts of your life you'd like by adhering to the straightforward procedures I'm about to share with you. The first step is to pick an area of your life where you want to gain more confidence. Create activities that get harder and harder in stage two. They should span the gamut from the most important thing you want to feel secure doing in the future to what you can do now if you just push yourself a little bit. After that, in step three, you begin working out in your growth zone. You repeat the process once the exercises become simple enough.

## *If it doesn't challenge you, it doesn't change you.*

When you do, you'll notice that some of the exercises that were once in your panic zone are now ones you can start working on in the growth zone. And one of those things will eventually be the major task you want to feel confident completing. Pretty basic, yes? Let's now have a look at an illustration of what that may entail. Let's assume that Umesh wishes to gain more confidence when speaking in front of groups so that he can contribute to meetings, make presentations, or lead seminars.

*"True self-discovery begins where your comfort zone ends." -Adam Braun*

Today, though, Umesh finds it difficult to even speak in meetings if there are more than a few attendees. Umesh's actions in this scenario might resemble these. He states that his first goal is to feel comfortable speaking in front of a sizable crowd. He develops some exercise suggestions in phase two. When someone in a huge group says something he agrees with, one thing he believes he can start doing today is to start saying "yeah" and "I agree" in a clear and concise manner.

*"Resistance to change is very much governed by your comfort zone. Just because something is comfortable does not for a moment mean it's what you want, or even good for you for that matter." -Robin H. C*

Asking simple questions in those bigger groups, such as "Can you repeat that?", is one that could be a bit more difficult but that he believes he can do at least occasionally. The task of creating and giving a brief, one-to three-minute presentation could be just on the other side of his panic zone. It's likely that the concept of spending one minute presenting anything to the group has slid just inside of Umesh's Growth Zone after he becomes confident in both stating his yeses and asking his questions. Now, keep in mind that Umesh could occasionally want to back out of performing these workouts. That's quite natural, and our superego—which we'll talk about in the next video—usually produces it. But as long as he can continue the practise despite these emotions, despite the superego, and without inducing a panic attack, he will eventually succeed in his endeavour.

*"A ship is always safe at the shore-but that is not what it is built for." -Albert Einstein*

We begin to step outside of our comfort zone and gain confidence when we take action despite feeling anxious or stressed out. You have to go through this process for yourself and come up with at least one activity that you can perform later today or tomorrow as your workout for this chapter. There is no need to hold off. You'll get where you want to go more quickly if you begin to build your confidence as soon as possible.

*"Coming out of your comfort zone is tough in the beginning, chaotic in the middle, and awesome in the end...because in the end, it shows you a whole new world."*
*-Manoj Arora*

Step outside your comfort zone and give something new a try. It might be something little, like trying a new meal, picking up a new hobby, or changing your bus route; or it can be something huge, like studying in a different area, picking up a new skill, or going to a foreign nation that you've never been to. Make your room a place you enjoy being in. The same for your workstation at work. Get rid of everything that is impeding your productivity. It should be surrounded by things that motivate and encourage you.

*"No one likes to move beyond their comfort zone, but as the saying goes, that's where the magic happens. It's where we grow, learn, and develop in a way that expands our horizons beyond what we thought was possible." -Andy Molinsky*

Each of us has a dream identity that we aspire to. What would your ideal self do? How can you begin to be your ideal self right away? You can do considerably more with the help of role models than you can on your own. Oprah Winfrey has personally inspired me due to the millions of lives she has touched, among other things. They inspire me to reach new heights because what I see in them and what they accomplish serves as a reminder of who I am and what I am capable of.

*"Face the fear, even if it's only a tiptoe outside of your comfort zone instead of a leap. Progress is progress."*
*-Annette White*

Having someone work with you on your objectives is the only way to progress more quickly. They'll not only inspire you to work harder, but they'll also give you sound advice you can use to further your own success. Many of my clients want me to coach them, and as a consequence, they make a lot more progress and have far better outcomes than they would have if they had worked on their own. As you learn more, develop more, and improve, you get better.

*"Life will only change when you become more committed to your dreams than you are to your comfort zone." -Billy Cox*

Being at a high awareness level means being able to get above fear-based responses and make thoughtful decisions that benefit both you and those around you. There will always be blind spots that we cannot see, no matter how hard we attempt to identify them. When we solicit comments, we can see ourselves from a different viewpoint. I completely agree with what Dan Steven once Said, "The comfort zone is the great enemy to creativity; moving beyond it necessitates intuition, which in turn configures new perspectives and conquers fears."

You may talk to your friends, family, coworkers, employer, or even acquaintances because they don't have any preconceived notions and can offer unbiased criticism.Establish passive income sources to ensure that your income is unrelated to the amount of time you spend working. Without a doubt, you'll keep working, but only because you want to, not because you have to. Helping others grow is the best way to develop yourself. In the end, there is only one planet. We are all on the same life journey. Either you can focus on the large picture or you may become bogged down in the minute details. The former will enable you to experience life far more fully than the latter.

***"I will guarantee you that the day you step outside your comfort zone by making success your goal, is the day you discover that adversity, risk, and daring will make life sweeter than you ever imagined." -Mark Burnett***

*Making the most of any situation that comes your way is a spiritual journey, no matter what someone else tosses at you.*

One day, an old donkey or as fell into a well after slipping. The well was not very deep and had dried up, but the donkey was unable to exit. It started wailing piteously from underneath. The owner and a few people arrived to see the incident. The donkey kept yelling, desperate to escape and terrified for its life. "This foolish donkey will keep shouting," someone said. We can neither use it for work nor sell it because it is already outdated and useless. Anyhow, we wished to plug the well. Now let's get to it. They made the decision to bury the donkey alive after sealing the well. They started filling the well with soil. The donkey would shake off any soil that accidentally landed on its back and stand on top of the mound. The earth continued to rise as it collected. It emerged from the well as soon as they had filled one side of it. The people thought this was a really clever ass. The owner went to the donkey and made an attempt at a hug in thanks. He received a direct kick to the face before fleeing for safety.

Even though it lacks a brain like yours, a mango tree can transform muck into fruit and sweetness. Plants are able to transform squalor into fragrant blossoms. You ought to be able to transform whatever is presented to you into something lovely. If you can achieve it, it demonstrates who you are. The largest issue on earth is that when little things go wrong, people tend to blame "the little guy" (someone else). They don't appear to be in charge of anything themselves. Stop placing blame or making excuses for other people. Instead, you should strive to reach your full potential.

*The most stupid thing to do is to look outside of yourself for something that only exists within you.*

People are gazing skyward in search of happiness and calm. They are searching the entire planet for happiness. It will only occur if you turn inside. We all have our own limitations and comfort zones. Most of us don't frequently leave this since we feel comfortable and secure in our familiar surroundings.The finest professional and personal experiences we may occasionally have, though, come from entirely stepping outside of our comfort zones. We know we attempted something new and probably learnt a lot in the process, even if it was an abysmal failure.

*How do you deal with challenging relationships?*

Is there anything more annoying than managing a problematic relationship? like a difficult coworker or a critical in-law? But doing so is essential to keeping a good mindset. Try using the step-back method to do this. As in, take a step back and think about these issues before resuming that difficult relationship. Stop trying to change tough individuals and give them room to be who they are. Instead of attempting to change people, concentrate on altering your interaction with them. Waiting to approach a tough individual won't help. Accept accountability for the connection. Keep things from becoming worse. Make contact to explore your differences and to learn more about one another. Talk to the individual, not about them. Put your ego aside, since that can be the problem. Be aware of how egos can enter the picture and exacerbate conflict. You should alter your strategy to prevent more egotistical assaults on them while maintaining self-control.

> *"Whenever you feel uncomfortable, instead of retreating back into your old comfort zone, pat yourself on the back and say, "I must be growing," and continue moving forward." – T. Harv Eker*

I previously had a problematic coworker who, in my opinion, continually questioned my competence and authority. But once I understood that my ego was exaggerating the circumstance, I was able to connect with him in a calmer, more detached way without rubbing my ego in his face. Assume that the tough person interacts with you for a purpose, and instead of closing down, which is a natural response, attempt to understand it by asking questions. Now, keeping this in mind also helps. We all have something to love, something to lose, and something to fear. Fear is the root of a lot of bad behaviour.

Is the difficult person behaving badly because they fear rejection, failure, or change? We all have the ability to love and be loved by someone or something. So even though you may not love the unpleasant person you're dealing with, they are loved. And in order to be liked, one must possess attributes that are admirable. Increase your capacity for love and seek out what others find admirable about that person. Instead of seeing them for what you perceive to be their flaws, try to see them for what they are to someone else. Perhaps a loved one has passed away. Perhaps their confidence or professional momentum has diminished. You know, the possibilities demand sympathy.

Examine your response to challenging situations first. Are you responding excessively and escalating the conflict? Are you handling an issue with composure, objectivity, and optimism? It is necessary to cease assuming bad intent. Never presume what someone else has in mind. Once more, attempt to comprehend the reasons behind their actions. Rarely do difficult people, including you, view themselves in that manner. You've undoubtedly encountered that challenging individual before. As was already established, these are typically totally acceptable explanations for challenging conduct. Build a few little bridges. Little gestures of goodwill, compassion, affirmation, and empathy go a long way toward repairing a relationship. Make an attempt to construct these bridges. Find tiny, sincere praises to give, for instance, and discover your areas of commonality. Don't fight; just demonstrate that you can be relied upon.

You are aware that, in the end, you get to decide how much influence you give problematic individuals. Don't allow one bad connection to overshadow all the amazing, good relationships you have in your life. Many of the good things in your life may be overshadowed by difficult relationships. So, to advance, take a step back.

## What do you hope people will remember you for?

"Legacy" is a popular term. Everyone aspires to make their mark and do something that will last a long time. Nobody desires to be overlooked. But how would you like to be recalled? Some people leave legacies they regret leaving behind because they are implicated in cover-ups, engage in scandals, or perhaps just plain let their family down. You don't have to be that. What you do now will decide if it is feasible for you to be remembered in 100 years—and to be remembered favourably. The qualities of humility, nobility, self-sacrifice, and consideration of others provide the best chance of achieving that sort of immortality.

*"Apart from values and ethics which I have tried to live by, the legacy I would like to leave behind is a very simple one - that I have always stood up for what I consider to be the right thing, and I have tried to be as fair and equitable as I could be."-Ratan Tata*

Even if people don't talk about legacies in casual conversation, practically everyone wonders about them on quiet rights. Especially for those of us who have reached milestones in our lives like maturity, middle age, and retirement. Have you ever observed a butterfly undergoing metamorphosis? Its emergence from its cocoon is painful and challenging. You could believe you're helping it by slicing the top of its chrysalis so it can emerge more easily.

*"Legacy is not leaving something for people. It's leaving something in people." - Peter Strople*

However, if you do that, the butterfly won't have fully formed wings and will be handicapped for the remainder of its life. Metamorphosis requires difficulties and struggles to occur. They are essential for both leaving a legacy and building one. This list of suggestions for starting with developing and building a legacy may be exactly the right step in the right path for you. People continue living regardless of their current circumstances for the fundamental reason that they have a purpose in life. With such a goal, life becomes manageable and even pleasurable. This collection of thoughts is intended for people who see the value of leaving a legacy but are unsure of why they should do so.

*"The purpose of life is not to be happy. It is to be useful, to be honorable, to be compassionate, to have it make some difference that you have lived and lived well." - Ralph Waldo Emerson*

People from all around the world are becoming more aware of the value of a good person in their society in preserving social ecological balance, preventing serious misconduct, and averting major conflicts. Good behaviour may be much easier to achieve if a person is built on a sense of shared values and purpose, even though it is crucial for him or her to have deterrent measures in place, such as legal procedures and social justice.

*"Be as light as a feather and when they reach for you — you will blow right by their grip; you will effortlessly flow to safety." — Bryant McGill*

People who act morally not out of concern for negative consequences but rather because it is consistent with their shared values and goals. In conclusion, a strong moral character that fosters success is built on a foundation of shared objectives. People who live in a society that is built on a sense of shared values and purpose do the right thing not out of concern for negative consequences but rather because it is in accordance with those values and purpose.

*"If you wanna make the world a better place, take a look at yourself, then make that change." – Michael Jackson*

You need to learn more profound information, like: what is the true nature of the being you refer to as "I"? What is the underlying force that has shaped the person reading this right now? What enthuses you and fills you with rapture? These are hints as to what your soul truly values in order to have a meaningful existence. What is most important? What really is important?

It is the duty of the deliberate life to honour that desire and identify what really feeds, what really summons development, as well, and then share that bigger expression of soul with others.

Living a life with more thought. You possess a lofty desire that is desperate to be realised and expressed. You have the capacity to be a source of possibility. You are a source of potential with unbounded potential. Your life will change if you think about these words for the next 30 days. I am aware that you might not perceive yourself the same way I do. I don't just view you as a human reading words on a screen; I see you as a soul. Beyond the self-perceptions you have, I sense your potential.

Many people think that confidence is something that comes with success, but the truth is that confidence is what actually brings about success. Our own minds and egos are where we get our confidence from. Therefore, developing our thinking is the most effective and simple technique to increase our confidence.

Adversity contains the seeds of success. In any circumstance, we must search for untapped potential. Due to the potential to express a prejudiced perspective, we must refrain from making snap decisions. Have you ever attempted to rush anything and had it crumble on you? Before the light bulb was finally created by Thomas Edison, 10,000 other designs were tried and failed. What must develop in its own timeframe cannot be rushed. Living effortlessly acknowledges collaboration with life's energies. If you have a tendency to move too quickly through life, consider patience as a virtue. What are you losing by moving too quickly? A hamster running on a wheel understands that the harder it runs, the slower it moves toward its destination. Switch to the leisurely road instead of the hamster wheel; everything that needs to happen will automatically do so. Examine the underlying cause if you need to move quickly. What do you want to avoid? If life slows down, what are you frightened of seeing? which you do not have control over? Keep your mind open to fresh perspectives, doors, and experiences that bring in welcome change. People who complain that life is boring reject this aspect of it. Even though it may be obscure to you, your existence in this space-time continuum is proof of your greatness.

Imagine what might happen if your passion and mission coincided!

- Have you ever thought about your life's purpose?
- What do you feel strongly about?
- What if you awoke each day with a strong desire to live your life?
- Do you ever have feelings of being lost or lacking anything in your life?

- Do you ever consider your options for living?
- How do you continually bring your best self forward?
- Why do individuals succeed sometimes and fail at other times?
- What must be prioritised in order to be most effective?
- If you had some guidance, would life be simpler?
- Do you believe your abilities exceed what your findings indicate?
- Do several anxieties weigh you down?
- Do they prevent you from leading the greatest life possible?
- But what if worrying has some advantages?

*Your mental state, your thoughts, forming wonderful connections with other people, and making wonderful memories are what bring you the most joy.*

The good news is that you can improve your life in a variety of tiny, straightforward ways. Multiple ways to improve your well-being, assist those around you, and offer yourself the opportunity to live your best life. These ideas could be a wonderful place to start, but only you truly know what adjustments in your life need to be made. Unfollow those that make you feel bad. You know, the one on Facebook who never stops moaning, the one on Twitter who is constantly debating you, or the Instagram influencer who is so flawless that it makes you feel awful about yourself? Right this second, unlock your phone, and unfollow them. You are not in need of that.

We all experience fears. Fear of danger, fear of public speaking, and fear of uncertainty all serve to keep us stagnant and stop us from progressing. Recognise that your worries are the compass for progress rather than avoiding them. Address them and go through them. Check out these four reasons to conquer fear. Make the most of your heart, soul, intellect, and body. You must optimise your mental, physical, emotional, and spiritual well-being in order to live your best life.

You are not living your life to the fullest if you are extremely successful, wealthy, socially connected, and spiritually attuned, yet you ignore your physical health. Likewise, in other circumstances where you "shut off" a portion of yourself. You are the only one you can change. Give up expecting others to act a specific way. Focus on changing yourself rather than putting pressure on everyone around you to do the same. This will make you happier and help you have a fuller life. Express your gratitude. Be appreciative of all you have now and will acquire in the future. Express your gratitude Make sure the folks who have impacted you are aware of your thanks. You'll be astonished at the impact a small deed like this can have. They won't know if you don't tell them.

*Life is always about aspiring for better, and if you aspire for the best, chances are you will get that and more.*

What do you hope people will remember you for? Since this is such a complex subject, I'll be honest and say that it was much harder than I anticipated to put it into words. This is the type of query that caused me to reflect deeply for a number of hours before writing this piece. But weirdly, it's something that has been on my mind a lot lately after dealing with the deaths of my grandpa only weeks apart. What do I want people to remember me for, then? Well, a number of ideas crossed my head, some surface-level and some rather profound. But as I continued to think and think, there were really just two things that kept coming to me. Two things were very important. I want to be known as a kind and nice person. I want people to remember me for my humanitarianism. I really think that compassion outshines all. Kindness, in my opinion, has the power to change people's lives, mend broken hearts, and unquestionably help others. However, whether or not I am recognised for it, I want to be known as someone who is kind, sympathetic, and helpful rather than just as someone who does these things. Assisting strangers who become friends in achieving their goals; assisting my family in overcoming difficulties and problems; and everything in between.

*"Twenty years from now you will be more disappointed by the things you didn't do than by the things you did." –*
*Mark Twain*

Many people pause at some point in their careers to wonder how they might influence others' futures and whether they are leaving a legacy. According to Charles Dickens, "No one who eases another person's suffering is useless in this life." Let's get right to the subject of creating a company legacy! For as long as there have been humans, legacies have played a significant role in society.

According to research, people are more inclined to make long-term-focused judgments when they have benefited from the legacy of a previous generation. Making a legacy a priority can also help to persuade powerful individuals to act morally.

*The desire to have a long-lasting impact on others is what drives people to leave a legacy.*

According to research, when individuals think about the long term, social duty is more important to them. The theme of legacy is about reflecting on the past, embracing the present, and laying the foundation for the future. Which is preferable for planting young trees: an open field or a clearing in an old-growth forest?

**"The important thing is not to stop questioning. Curiosity has its own reason for existing. One cannot help but be in awe when one contemplates the mysteries of eternity, of life, of the marvellous structure of reality. It is enough if one tries to comprehend only a little of this mystery every day."- Albert Einstein**

The theory of relativity was created by the German theoretical physicist Albert Einstein who won the Nobel Prize. Additionally, the renown eccentric genius created the mass-energy equivalency equation, $E = mc2$. Although his theory of relativity is what made him most famous, his genius extended beyond that. With his Nobel Prize-winning research on the photoelectric effect, he contributed to the development of quantum mechanics and helped usher in the atomic age, despite his overall opposition to the use of nuclear weapons. He established the law of the photoelectric effect, for which he was awarded the Nobel Prize in Physics in 1921.

It doesn't matter where you start, only where you finish. Staying true to what you believe can be the most enduring portion of your legacy.

A large portion of the study of the universe's development as well as contemporary technologies, such as lasers and computer chips, were made possible thanks to Einstein's efforts. Generations of brilliant minds will continue to be inspired by his eternal influence. His objective was to develop a "Grand Unified Theory" that would encompass all physical events, from the tiniest subatomic particles to the entire cosmos. The search for the Grand Unified Theory, however, remains one of the most actively researched areas of physics today, so Einstein's ambition did not perish with him.

*"Our days are numbered. One of the primary goals in our lives should be to prepare for our last day. The legacy we leave is not just in our possessions, but in the quality of our lives. What preparations should we be making now?*

*The greatest waste in all of our earth, which cannot be recycled or reclaimed, is our waste of the time that God has given us each day." — Bill Graham*

His findings transformed how we view not only our planet but the entire cosmos. The cosmos as we know it was redefined by Einstein's work, which also provided us with the most understandable, elegant model to date. Black holes, the biggest cosmic monsters among them, and gravitational lensing have been discovered thanks to the theoretical physics foundation he established. He laid foundation for the development of quantum theory. It's hardly surprising that Einstein's name has come to represent scientific brilliance. The brilliance of Albert Einstein is difficult to overstate. He was one of the most prominent physicists in the world. Generations of brilliant minds will continue to be inspired by his eternal influence.

*"Your mind is for having ideas, not holding them."*
*-David Allen*

Living in the now and making decisions for the present while being cognizant of an uncertain future is one of the biggest challenges facing humans. Being aware of our mortality is the dilemma's most extreme example. But we frequently face situations in life where we must make crucial judgments with little knowledge. One key aspect of the human experience is the underlying ambiguity of the future. We make an effort to live a decent, meaningful life despite the fact that we can never be certain of what is ahead for us. Nobody can live just in the now while ignoring the future. There must be a weekly rhythm and a link to a greater purpose. There must be a generational rhythm as well as a seasonal rhythm.

> *"You can't leave a footprint that lasts if you're always walking on tiptoe." - Marion Blakey*

According to ecologists, young trees thrive when placed near more mature ones. The new tree's roots are able to follow the trails left by older trees, which allows them to establish themselves more deeply, it would appear. The new tree's roots are able to follow the trails left by older trees, which allows them to establish themselves more deeply, it would appear. The roots of many trees may really graft together over time, forming a complex, interconnected foundation under the earth. Stronger trees help weaker ones out by sharing resources in order to improve the health of the entire forest. That is legacy: a connection through time, a need for those who came before us, and a duty to those who will follow. Being human is essential to the essence of being human. Adults lose significance in their lives when, according to research, they don't feel like they are trying to leave a legacy.

> *"Life is not easy for any of us. But what of that? We must have perseverance and above all confidence in ourselves. We must believe that we are gifted for something and that this thing must be attained." -Marie Curie*

Marie Curie, a physicist and chemist, paved the way for women in science. She overcame obstacles and gave new concepts life. Her remarkable career is dotted with firsts, including becoming the first woman to win two Nobel Prizes, the first to have a daughter receive the prize, and many other noteworthy distinctions. Marie Curie, the first recipient of the award in two distinct categories, produced ground-breaking scientific discoveries. The groundbreaking radiation study that the Polish scientist and chemist conducted made her renowned. She conducted the initial studies into using radiation to cure tumours after discovering the two new substances, radium and polonium. But what is truly amazing is that she continued her studies during a period when she was sometimes the only female present. She stresses the value of representation and diversity in the STEM professions. We all gain when people with various identities and origins are included in science. Curie's more than 100-year-old break in the glass ceiling is even more remarkable when you consider the gender disparity that still exists today.

*"We should not allow it to be believed that all scientific progress can be reduced to mechanisms, machines, gearings, even though such machinery also has its beauty. Neither do I believe that the spirit of adventure runs any risk of disappearing in our world."- Marie Curie*

Many would concur that the path toward better representation may not have been feasible without Curie's earlier attempts, even if there are still many advancements to be achieved. Without a doubt, Marie Curie was a trailblazer who paved the way for women in science. She was hailed as a "celebrity scientist" throughout her lifetime. In addition to her achievements, we should honour scientists for the boldness and determination it takes to make any kind of discovery. There are courageous workers doing their jobs right now. Although scientists have done all of those things, they are bold because undertaking something no one has ever done before entails significant emotional risks. What will you do to leave your imprint on the world now that they have all done so? Making a difference can always be done at any time.

*"You cannot hope to build a better world without improving the individuals. To that end, each of us must work for his own improvement and, at the same time, share a general responsibility for all humanity, our particular duty being to aid those to whom we think we can be most useful."-Marie Curie*

Most people believe that a legacy is something you leave behind or something good that happens to other people after you have lived your life. Knowing your final aim is necessary for building anything. What does leaving a living legacy mean to you? What do you hope to contribute to the world? You may be experiencing a significant societal shift or improvement that affects a sizable populace. It's also possible that your legacy will have a greater influence on a smaller group and a more personal reach. The issue of what you want your living legacy to be has no right or incorrect response. Many successful individuals I know live their legacy by giving back monetarily and by creating initiatives and materials that encourage others to be their best selves. I want to live my legacy while I'm still here because I don't want to wait until I'm gone to have the biggest influence.

*"Immortality is to live your life doing good things, and leaving your mark behind." —Brandon Lee*

Act now to establish your living legacy. Whatever you want your living legacy to be, start right away. Do something, however tiny. You are genuinely living your legacy today if you take any action that advances it. Your effect will be stronger the longer you can live out your legacy. There is no certainty that you will spend any time on earth. This implies that in order to have the greatest influence, you must live your legacy each and every day that you are given the gift of breathing. Any activity may be successful if you are consistent. Single deeds and legacy-making moments add up to a lasting legacy. Be certain about the steps you will take to establish your living legacy when you get up every day. Be tenacious Resistance has always been present in great attempts. This may come to you as immediate feedback from others around you or as part of the everyday rigours of a life filled with distractions.

## Self-Assessment Questions:

- You may use these questions to choose the legacy you want to leave:
- What values do you want to live by?
- How do you want your loved ones and friends to remember you?
- What will people remember you for outside of your immediate family and close friends?
- What sort of influence do you hope to have on your neighbourhood?
- How will your presence in the world make it a better place?
- What improvements do you want to make to your field?
- What people will you have an impact on?
- What knowledge would you wish to impart to the next generation?

- What do you wish to depart with?

The methods listed below will help you decide what legacy you want to leave behind when you pass away. How to Leave a Legacy? Use the following concepts as a starting point to generate legacy-building ideas. Expand your understanding of the area. Through your body of work, you can leave a legacy. Here are some suggestions on how you might develop your own living legacy and ideas on how to be remembered in 100 years.

- Have a legacy driven mind simply means using your unique talents in a way that benefits society as a whole while also having personal significance for you. It's helpful to ask yourself what you are good at in order to identify what you care about. What talents do you have that may be applied to a good cause? What in the neighbourhood has significance for you? You will discover your interests and how your passions might give your life purpose by thinking about and responding to these questions.
- Do not let others' opinions affect your ability to trust yourself. The values and fundamental beliefs of people who lead meaningful lives shape their decisions and establish their short-and long-term priorities. It is what directs and moulds their daily behaviour. Although it's common to follow social conventions, there is no right or wrong way to spend your life.
- You may live your life guilt-free and be able to choose what is best for you if you trust your instincts and listen to your intuition. You must learn to trust yourself and your capacity to make the decisions that are best for you if you want to have a meaningful life.

- Motivate others one of the biggest benefits of living a life with a purpose is that you may feel proud of yourself while serving your community and learning more about your talents and abilities. If you lack this self-awareness, you cannot teach people how to help others.
- Although physical prowess is not necessary, it does call for strong feelings and convictions that may be channelled towards empowering others. You will be able to inspire others to assist others via their own personal benefits and pass it on by leading a meaningful life.
- Giving folks the confidence and freedom to pursue their lives without the constraints of surviving by appeasing someone else will inspire them to do the same for other people. Because of your words and deeds, others will feel better about themselves, which will spread positivity to others. It's a never-ending loop of good things.
- Even though life is never simple, it may be made simpler if you can learn to let go of failure and be satisfied with your goals. Your life will only get more difficult if you decide to pursue a path that isn't in line with your purpose.
- It's crucial to go past your setbacks and find happiness in where you are right now. For instance, declining a job that contradicts your ideals or involves tasks that challenge your self-confidence doesn't make you a loser. On the contrary, it implies that your life's purpose extends beyond success and wealth. It indicates that you are fulfilled and aware of your life's mission. Power is not as significant as having inner serenity and faith in oneself.
- Additionally, you may make a scrapbook for your loved ones, a website devoted to your legacy, or record video

messages for them. Give your alma mater a scholarship so that future students can benefit. If you knew you didn't have long to live, write down everything you'd want to tell your loved ones in a legacy letter. Write about your life's lessons, values, successes, and goals to really convey who you are. Consider it a sentimental heirloom. Create a blog.

- Volunteer create a nonprofit or a business from scratch. Create a memoir. Handmade objects like quilts, cedar hope boxes, or woodwork crafts should be passed on. Start a new initiative in your neighbourhood, such as a recycling campaign, a community garden, or a playground. Impart knowledge and skills. Develop your abilities, recognise your strengths, and be loyal to who you are. You may start writing a book also.

- By leaving money to your heirs, you can provide them with a solid foundation on which to build their futures. Giving money to causes close to your heart by leaving a bequest note down the family's customs and recipes.

Finally, your legacy will continue to expand and spread. There is no greater illustration of this than the numerous new versions of books that have been released after their initial release or publication when the writers' thoughts and knowledge have advanced. As you change, your legacy will as well. After a few years, I have a greater understanding and appreciation of why I set out to create this after utilising, discussing, and listening to customers' experiences, and I will continue to be open to what new insights may surface. Whatever is going on in your life, concentrating on the things you are grateful for might change your perspective.

*"No matter what happens in life, be good to people. Being good to people is a wonderful legacy to leave behind."-Taylor Swift.*

Making a legacy proactively is likewise non-egocentric. It is soul-driven and is simple to identify by the urge to "give back," to advance things, to share — a natural progression in service to others. My desire to create a coaching resource turned into a persistent nagging thought. Another day with a lot of possibility and opportunity is tomorrow. You should start it over completely and from scratch. Spend 10 minutes every night organising the mess and preparing your house for the next day. Your future self will appreciate it. One of the best presents we have ever received is today. Let's make good use of it and avoid throwing any away.

*"If you would not be forgotten as soon as you are dead, either write something worth reading or do something worth writing." —Benjamin Franklin*

The greatest way to have the most influence is to share your contribution with the entire world, even if not everyone is born with an instinctive desire to be in the spotlight. Tell everyone what your legacy is. Start with your family and friends, but watch out for those who may react negatively. Make sure you have a strong support system around you while you build your living legacy. Live your own self-authentic existence. You could be shocked by how the world reacts if you share from the heart and offer the world your gift. The Lesson We all have the capacity to make a difference when we enter this world. Why wait until after your death for your effect to be felt, whatever it may be? By taking action and allowing the world to gain from you and your contribution, you may establish your living legacy. We will experience the greatest effect when we are all carrying out our legacy.

*The marathon of living your legacy will take you over mountainous terrain and lovely pastures. Your path's course will contribute to how you establish your living legacy.*

# CHAPTER THREE

# Go Beyond Your Limitations And Rewrite Your Destiny

*"No one saves us but ourselves. No one can and no one may. We ourselves must walk the path."-Gautama Buddha*

*Understand your positive and negative emotions to leave a legacy.*

We all want to know that our lives have meaning and that we have made an impact on the world. How do you define leaving a leagacy? It entails leaving a mark on the future and giving back to subsequent generations. People want to feel as though their lives mattered, which is why they want to leave a legacy. You may begin acting in the manner in which you wish to be remembered. You'll be able to start doing what matters right away. You can spend your time and other resources more wisely if you know what you want your legacy to be. It will positively affect the decisions you make every day. Clarity over your desired legacy may offer your life significance and direction. You'll be able to use the legacy you're leaving to guide how you interact with others every day. You'll conduct your life as though it matters.

## *How do you decide to be optimistic?*

Life is full of change, and while many people believe that change always results in bad things, you must make the conscious decision to perceive change as something that is occurring to you rather than for you. I've been there; to you, it implies that you're trapped, that it's unfair, and that you're acting the victim. For you, this entails embracing change as a way to promote growth and optimism in your life. So, if you can't alter the circumstances, try improving how you see them.

Sometimes it's challenging to maintain a happy attitude. Work-related frustrations, current affairs, personal setbacks, and other forms of pessimism may all weigh down your outlook, presence, and potential. Nevertheless, despite everything, you may continue to be positive by choosing to do so, not by accident. You must decide on three key issues in particular. The first step is to decide to look forward. It's common for people to feel awful or depressed occasionally, but even when things aren't going well and it seems like you're going backward, you must always keep pushing forward.

Positive thinking fuels all forward movement, even baby steps. It's challenging to move forward, but this will help. Big picture, tiny step is a phrase you should repeat to yourself when you're struggling to maintain your optimistic perspective despite obstacles. In other words, to inspire yourself, revisit your big image, the picture of the life you want to lead, the life that is currently difficult to envision. Then, consider what is the simplest move you can do to begin moving once more in the direction of your larger goal.

According to research, even simply taking the initial step can have a big impact since it starts the positive feedback loop of advancement. Consider the scenario where you were a strong candidate for the job in your ideal field but someone else who was more qualified won. You may go into a downward cycle as a result of the setback, or you could think "large vision, little step." Then, you image yourself working in that sector, and you decide on the first baby step you can do to get back on track, such as asking the interviewer how you can improve for the following chance.

## *Life has a natural rhythm; everything moves in a complex pattern, as seen in a flock of birds flying and diving together.*

Since life will take care of everything in due course, you don't need to cling to anything. Lao Tzu, a philosopher from China, is credited with saying that "Nature does not haste, but all is completed." To produce a flawless result, each condition retains its own self-organising system. Everything functions well without any unneeded anxiety.

***"If your emotional abilities aren't in hand, if you don't have self-awareness, if you are not able to manage your distressing emotions, if you can't have empathy and have effective relationships, then no matter how smart you are, you are not going to get very far."-Daniel Goleman***

Jessica Cox, a pilot with no arms who learned to fly with her feet. Due to a rare birth abnormality, Jessica Cox was born without arms. She has continued to live her life to the fullest despite this. Ms. Cox has really accomplished and experienced more than most individuals do in a lifetime.

She started her pilot training after earning her degree from the University of Arizona in 2005. According to CNN, Cox, a motivational speaker who can play the piano, drive a vehicle, scuba dive, and even hold a third-degree black belt in karate, wants to inspire individuals with disabilities and has visited more than 20 countries. She frequently considers what her life would be like if she could turn back time and be born with arms. Not only would her life be drastically different, but she would also understand how powerful it is to live one's life in a way that has such a profound effect on others. She has had leaders and role models. And now that she has experienced it, it's her duty to provide the same for the next generation of arms. She told the CNN news channel. Despite her initial dread of flying, Cox quickly overcame it and concentrated on obtaining her licence. Cox told the media outlet, "I had multiple flying instructors and contributed to my training to find this out." Therefore, determining what would work through trial and error took three years.

*If you believe you are not capable of anything, your mind will provide you with all the evidence that you are not.*

Because many people place restrictions on their own potential. I hope these sayings motivate you to pursue your aspirations and live a life without boundaries. "Exceeding boundaries and establishing your own rules is sometimes the greatest way to learn." Stop putting yourself at a disadvantage. Recognise that the possibilities for what you can do with your life are endless.

## *What does it mean to "put boundaries in place"?*

Why do we take them upon ourselves, exactly? When we create limits for ourselves, we determine that there are some things we are only capable of, certain distances we may travel, and certain things we only have a limited set of abilities. Why did we make this decision? Where did these concepts come from? Frequently, we create them without any tests or evidence. They stem from feelings of dread or failure, from messages we received as children, or from the fact that we have allowed the limitations of others to affect us. Your mind is what you feed yourself, just as your body is what you consume. All facets of your life are affected negatively by your thoughts.

*Nothing can prevent you from succeeding and evolving into your greatest self if you train your mind and harness its immense potential. Have faith in your own potential, skills, and abilities. All of your hopes and dreams are attainable for you.*

Things only seem challenging before you try something new or start working toward a goal. When you overcome mental obstacles, you feel at ease performing tasks and discover that they are simpler than you had believed. The human mind is hard-wired for simplicity and takes the easiest route to keep you safe from harm. It would always pick comfort over unfamiliarity, pleasure over pain, and leisure over hard work.

Perhaps not many, but Smt. Draupadi Murmu, our 15th nation's president, has been through many catastrophes, including the loss of her husband and two of her sons. News sources state that one of her sons departed tragically in 2009 under strange circumstances, and that her second son perished in a car accident three years later. She had already lost her husband to cardiac arrest. Smt. Murmu reportedly experienced sadness and anxiety at one point, but she made the decision to rise above her personal setbacks and commit her life to social change and public service. Smt. Murmu sought solace from her misery by joining the BrahmKumari community and travelling the spiritual path.

*If you want to succeed, intelligence might be useful, but you also need to have dedication and mental toughness. Maintain your focus with these helpful behaviours.*

Smt. Draupadi Murmu is familiar with the harsh realities of life and the battle for existence faced by the average person. She has faced adversity in her life, but she has persevered by walking the public way without complaint. She overcame several obstacles to get her education despite being born into an average household. Smt. Draupadi Murmu is a representation of the strong Indian woman who overcomes numerous obstacles in life. Her fight against hardships and personal tragedies has been continuous and protracted. She overcame them and added adventure to her life. She has experience working in state secretariats; serving two terms in the legislature; serving as a minister in Odisha; and serving as an effective governor in a state with a predominance of tribalism. Smt. Draupadi Murmu's election as India's president will greatly advance women's rights. This is an occasion to congratulate Smt. Draupadi

Murmu, who has been elected as our nation's second female president and first tribal woman. Being elected president, she represents the genuine beauty of her inspirational life path, which was filled with highs and lows, tragedies, and losses.

*"Always be yourself and have faith in yourself. Do not go out and look for a successful personality and try to duplicate it." -Bruce Lee*

The human mind is hard-wired for simplicity and takes the easiest route to keep you safe from harm. It would always pick comfort over unfamiliarity, pleasure over pain, and leisure over hard work. It is essential to have a development attitude in order to push your boundaries. When you adopt a development mentality, you clearly communicate to your subconscious that nothing is out of your reach. You can learn anything you're enthusiastic about, develop your talents, and become whatever it is you want to be.

There are no restrictions of any kind. Your mind starts to see the bridges instead of the streams, the solutions instead of the issues, and the road ahead instead of the hurdles with the appropriate sort of programming. The fundamental shift in how you view yourself that the growth mindset causes is what makes you unique and unlocks the doors to your future success. You must push past your limitations and leave your comfort zone in order to achieve your objectives and become the person you desire. Eleanor Roosevelt once stated, "You must do the things you believe you cannot do." You only become aware of your potential when you push past your limitations.

*"The only limit to your impact is your imagination and commitment." – Tony Robbins*

As a result, you must flip the narrative and prepare your mind, teaching it to do what you desire. It's all in your head in the end, whether you succeed or fail, fight or give up, or live an ordinary or remarkable life. You must make the necessary effort. However, you must first let go of any mental restrictions and have confidence in your ability to bring your aspirations to reality. Your world is created by what you think and visualise in your head. When you have confidence in yourself, you'll start to attract opportunities, your skills will advance, and your chances of success will dramatically improve. You must understand that your inner world determines what you manifest in your outer environment. Since your inner world determines what you manifest in your outer environment, you must plant the seeds of positive thought if you want your efforts to have a positive result. Despite all of the opposition, justifications, and weak arguments, you must be proactive and take action. Just get going. Any worthwhile goal must be pursued with zeal.

## *What is the meaning of life?*

One of the foundational elements of happiness is having a purpose in life.

It will be more difficult to achieve lasting pleasure without a purpose, but that doesn't imply you can't be happy without one. What are some examples of a life purpose?

There are several well-known goals in life, including: How to determine your own life's purpose? How to make sure you remain on path and finish what you started when the unexpected occurs! There are a lot of suggestions to help you determine what you want in life in general! You won't ever run out of life-altering thoughts again. The most important step you must take to guarantee your success! Fortunately, this topic demonstrates how simple this is. Your systems determine how high you can fall. Here, you'll find a tried-and-true strategy that can help you succeed.

*You can't take someone else's life's purpose and try to live it yourself while expecting to be happy. You must identify and establish your own life purpose if you wish to have a meaningful life.*

Nick Vujicic was born with phocamelia, a rare congenital disorder characterised by limb deformity. He has overcome the odds despite having very little foot by becoming a motivational speaker, getting married, and becoming a new father to Kiyoshi. Nick shares that he was fortunate to be born without limbs and legs, showing remarkable humility and sensitivity. For him, coping entails finding out how to live without something they have always known, which is a far more difficult task. How was this all made possible?

I watch in awe as Nick tells tales that highlight significant events in his life. He is very grateful for a small foot (or chicken drumstick, as he fondly refers to it), which allows him to do a lot of things, like wash his teeth, drive a car, use a computer, and more. With what he has, he has been able to lead a self-sufficient existence, produce four books, and inspire others. He says that comparing oneself to those who are better, richer, or more attractive all throughout one's life would only lead to unhappiness.

Gratitude has always been associated with leading a fulfilled life. Robert Emmons' study has shown that being appreciative has substantial psychological, social, and physical advantages. Gratitude practitioners frequently report stronger immune systems, greater sleep, and happier dispositions. Additionally, they report feeling more kind and less alone.

The goal of Nick Vujicic, an evangelist and international speaker of Australian descent, and his team at Life Without Limbs is to overcome boundaries, tear down walls, and create bridges that connect people. He has inspired millions of people across the world despite his disability. Nick is an excellent role model for practically everyone who has faced the toughest obstacles in life and yet wants to achieve their biggest dreams.

> *A few injustices or tragedies may be more profound than denying someone the chance to strive or even hope because of a constraint that is imposed from without but is mistakenly believed to be from within.*

The You-Factor offers the secret to living the life of greatness you were meant to live by weaving together personal experiences, useful ideas, and profound biblical truth. Everyone wants success in their lives. However, we all define prosperity slightly differently. Some people interpret it as having plenty of money and being wealthy. Others believe that happiness begins with perfect health or freedom. The Prosperity factor is your road map to achieving your goal and personal dream of success.

> *Limitations only exist when you impose them on yourself mentally.*

If you give your mind pleasant thoughts and guide it in the proper path, it has limitless power. It may be trained to do whatever you wish. Your thinking and viewpoint are greatly influenced by the narratives you tell yourself and the images you envision in your head.

*"If you always out limits on everything you do, physical or anything else, it will spread into your work, and into your life. There are no limits. There are only plateaus, and you must go beyond them." – Bruce Lee*

Your actions are influenced by your ideas, which in turn mould your reality. The limit is in your head, said Arnold Schwarzenegger. He had always believed that "as long as the mind can envisage the notion that you can achieve anything, you can do it, as long as you believe 100 percent." And the outcome of that belief is plainly seen to everyone. The limits are all made up and fictitious in your imagination. They get stronger the more you cave in to them. The more you give in to them, the more control they exert over you as they get stronger. Many individuals go through life living in mediocrity because they accept limiting ideas and neglect to access their inner strength. The majority of the time, mental obstacles are false self-imposed ideas about oneself that cause self-sabotage.

*"Limits like fears are often just an illusion." Michael Jordan*

When you tell yourself what you can or cannot achieve without first determining what you are actually capable of, you become your worst energy. These unfounded presumptions put a stop to your progress and keep you from achieving your goals and ambitions. Consequently, you are doomed to a life of mediocrity.

You'll start to see answers and breakthroughs if you change your perspective and convince yourself that you can do anything. Ignore the negativity within and around you and make the decision to only think of good ideas. Do that repeatedly, despite your feelings of helplessness, dejection, and lack of motivation. By giving yourself encouragement, you may direct your inner energy toward good expectations and look forward to the results of your work. It is essential to have a development attitude in order to push your boundaries.

*"It is not a person or situation that affects your life; it is the meaning you give to that person or situation, which influences your emotions and actions. Your choice is to change the meaning you gave it or to change your response, in order to create the outcome you want."-Shannon L. Alder*

The meaning of life varies from person to person, just as happiness is something that is unique to every single person! While Elon Musk's goal in life may be to bring future concepts to life, yours may just be to give your family and kids the greatest possible existence. Many people succumb to their desires because they are guided by unconscious desires that they are unaware of.

We have a choice: we may accept the suffering of the world or we can make a conscious effort to think lovingly and compassionately every day. The hardest thing you have to do is learn to live with your ideas while not buying into the story they tell. Regardless of your level, money, or situation, I dare you to spend some time alone with your thoughts. They won't find their genuine selves until after that. On the one hand, we assert that we have free will, but our unconscious desires prevent us from using this freedom. Your worries and anxieties will lead you astray and should not be allowed to guide you. Be led by your creative thinking, which is where your intuitive mind resides. We can easily break the habit of paying attention to automatic ideas.

*Be strong enough to live the life you've always wanted, courageous enough to speak up, and brave enough to follow your heart.*

What do Oprah Winfrey, J.K. Rowling, Colonel Saunders, and Michael Jordan have in common? Despite challenging conditions, a lack of resources, other people's lack of confidence in them, maltreatment, and financial challenges, they all overcame the odds to achieve their professional ambitions. How do you know when to stop trying or cut your losses? What distinguishes perseverance from kicking a dead horse? Maybe you've got a target in your sights that you want to work toward.

**"The finest emotion of which we are capable is the mystic emotion." -Albert Einstein**

However, you are not getting the outcomes you were hoping for. As you consider if this is only a setback or whether you should press forward in faith, uncertainty sets in that perhaps you are going about things the incorrect way. The choice to endure is one of the hardest ones to make, whether you decide to keep fishing in a certain area on the lake or stay in a bad marriage in the hopes that things will improve. When a change in strategy or direction is necessary, only you can decide. Only you can decide whether it is appropriate to put time and effort into a failed relationship or career endeavour. The trick is to change your behaviour rather than give up. As long as you keep trying, you will succeed.

*Everyone who wants to find a perfect companion may, with the exception of the one who gives up.*

Consider the following ideas to keep going when you're feeling discouraged and unsure when you've worked hard for success but only see evidence of the opposite. Don't you ever have the sense that your life is passing you by without you doing anything to enjoy it?

*Do you realise that you have already lived over half of your remaining life?*

- Live your life on your terms and spend less time trying to swim against the current.
- Follow the flow of life and keep an open mind.
- Realise that there are no mistakes as you take one stride forward and two steps back.

Your greatest gift comes from taking that one step back because it gives you the information and expertise you need to achieve your objective. Follow your passion, but don't be too set in your ways about how you'll get there.

*Success has several facets, including not only material wealth but also good physical, mental, and emotional health.*

Accept what seems to be a dead end as a blessing in disguise rather than fight it. Allow life to throw open doors and illuminate previously unimagined paths to your goals. Giving up is not surrendering. It is a step in the procedure.

It is an accepting state. Without the capacity to allow, you will not be able to persist.

*No matter how many people you encounter in your life, all that matters is finding the genuine ones who will love you for who you are and guide you toward becoming the person you should be.*

We require the ability to express ourselves freely as well as the ability to love and feel valued. Success in one area does not support the other. This explains why some individuals appear to have it all yet aren't actually content. We are all born with immense potential. We all have untapped potential that is just waiting to be fulfilled. We all have this emotion inside of us. The sadness is that by ignoring the manifestation of this creativity, we are doing the gravest imaginable offence. Unfortunately, these special abilities and skills become a poisonous, deadly force when they go undeveloped.

*"Only if you invest your emotions in what matters to you, will life become powerful and really meaningful."-*
*Sadguru*

We develop harmful behaviours as a result of this act of suppression, the main one of which is self-sabotage. We have been instructed to hold back our might and to cease believing in our natural instincts and fundamental wisdom. The weight placed upon us and its resultant impact on the amount of time we have to enjoy life keeps us helpless. Encourage joyful emotions finding meaning can be aided by cultivating good feelings like appreciation. Because caring for others, discovering your purpose in life, and general well-being are all correlated with happy feelings. You may be better able to concentrate on how you can make a difference in the world if you have a direct connection to your happy feelings.

Developing an attitude of thankfulness enables you to take stock of your benefits and spread them to others. This is frequently regarded as a case when someone may find "found" money. They give their newly discovered money to others as part of their blessing. A life lived with purpose and thankfulness might be characterised as being grateful for the ability to connect with things in life that aren't quantifiable and to distinguish between desires and necessities. The common positive emotions are love, serenity, forgiveness, awe, joy, interest, hope, pride, amusement, and inspiration.

## *Self-belief and hard work will always earn you success.*

You are inspired to undertake things that you previously believed were impossible for you when you believe in yourself. You can take the first step, the next one, and then another step because of your faith. Before you know it, you're walking briskly along the road that once gave you anxiety. With each encounter, when we truly pause to confront fear, we acquire strength, bravery, and confidence.

**"Positive emotions and mental states may make people more resilient to stress, like sturdy tree branches that bend but don't break when battered by a storm"-Melanie Greenberg**

We need to take action on what we believe we cannot. Why do individuals seem to be stuck in a cycle of trying and failing to succeed? Why is it that even after we successfully lose weight, deliver a stellar presentation, or land that job, we frequently regain the weight or continue to feel incompetent? Why does it occasionally cause us to lose everything we have worked so hard to accomplish? Having the proper mindset and beliefs is the first step in achieving any objective, whether it be managing weight, overcoming poor self-esteem, or landing the dream job.

Everyone is aware of Michael Phelps' exceptional athleticism. Few people are aware that he suffers from Attention Deficit Hyperactivity Disorder (ADHD), and swimming is how he manages the excess energy his body produces. Many people think ADHD is a bad affliction, but Michael used it as motivation to swim. He recognised his primary weakness and channelled it into his greatest strength. You can take inspiration from him and use your flaws as motivation to strive harder or smarter. Michael Phelps is constantly in top physical shape to pull off his victories. He keeps up excellent levels of fitness and has a fantastic body. He puts a lot of effort into his exercises and attributes his general skill to strong genetics.

More than most people, Michael Phelps is aware that success does not come easily. The most decorated Olympian in history, while becoming a standout at a young age, put in the necessary effort over the duration of his career. He is aware of the impact of perseverance and hard effort as well as the places that these qualities might lead. Nothing else is getting in the way of our achieving our objectives and desires. Continue to be inspired, hungry, and driven. He is renowned across the entire world for becoming the most decorated Olympian in history. Olympic swimmer Michael Phelps is one of them. He has won 28 Olympic medals in total. There are 23 gold medals among them. The most incredible part is how he managed to accumulate all of these in only five Olympics. Michael is widely recognised for using the butterfly as his preferred swimming stroke. At the age of 31, he made the decision to stop competing in professional swimming after many Olympic victories. However, he won 5 gold medals and 1 silver medal, bidding the Olympic pools a happy farewell. He has a brave, tenacious, and resolute narrative.

*"You can't put a limit on anything. The more you dream, the farther you get." -Michael Phelps*

Last but not least, the Phelps comment that is unquestionably the most well-known of all time and a favourite among fans. Given how frequently we have heard it (and read it) during our swimming careers, it may now feel like a cliche. But that is absolutely true. Michael Phelps points out that we are the only ones who have real limits.

When you are aware of the specific reason why your performance fell short of expectations, you get a particular feeling in the pit of your stomach. Give your best effort in order to avoid these emotions and all of the "what ifs" in order to do yourself a favour. Focus on the tasks you know you should do. Later on, you'll appreciate yourself. It's easy to occasionally go into a type of funk. It's simple to allow how your body feels to take control after a particularly challenging training session. You're feeling worn out and hurt, and you're unsure when the taper will start. But it's important to remember your initial motivations while you go through this unavoidable period. You set a goal for this season at the start of the year, whether you wrote it down or just had it in the back of your mind. It's not the right moment to stop pursuing it right now; instead, intensify your efforts.

This is not an easy one, and it gets even more difficult if you are working toward success in your endeavours. When things are difficult, your aspirations appear unattainable, and the circumstances are adverse, it is your conviction in yourself and your capacity to achieve your goals that keeps you going. When you have confidence in yourself, you work more diligently, passionately, and enthusiastically. You go into turbo mode because of the mental conditioning that says your efforts will pay off and you'll succeed; nothing can stop you from accomplishing your objectives. Your confidence will increase in direct proportion to how much you believe in yourself. You'll feel inspired to act, move beyond your comfort zone, seize new possibilities, take risks, and explore the unknown. Your confidence increases your self-assurance.

> *Self-belief is what motivates you to take action and won't let you give up until you achieve your goals.*

Self-belief is the first step toward success. You start on a good note and give yourself a head start when you have a strong sense of self-belief. Self-belief believes that you will succeed even before you start. You carry out all the actions of a champion because you behave and think like a successful person. As a result of your victory, your success has started to materialise.

Even if it's not always simple to get back up after an accident or failure, some people manage it and inspire others. When a horrific catastrophe or heartbreaking situation occurs, most people lose hope. However, some people never give up and go on to inspire millions of others. Yes, I'm referring to Muniba Mazari, a person who is confined to a wheelchair yet nevertheless motivates others and advances society.

Muniba claimed that her time in the hospital was the hardest time of her life since she had to rely on people for even a sip of water. She occasionally felt thirsty in the middle of the night, but she was forced to go the entire time without drinking anything since she didn't want to wake the others up. After spending two years in bed, she was given permission to use a wheelchair.

How to be grateful after difficulties, after a serious vehicle accident that left Muniba Mazari unable to walk, she chose to live her life rather than weep. There are many inspiring people in the world, and each one has a unique life narrative. This is the tale of a lady whose wonderfully flawed existence has shaped who she is now. This is the tale of a woman who holds the opinion that sometimes our issues aren't so large, but we're just not big enough to deal with them. Let's examine Muniba Mazari's remarkable life story and how she came to be in this position. Muniba Mazari asserts that words have the ability to either make or ruin a person. They have the power to either restore your soul or irreparably harm it. Muniba Mazari has watched her life fall apart in front of her eyes since she was a small child, yet she has never given up. Many people have illnesses that render them permanently crippled, but the first thing they do is give up. One of them is this incredible angel who showed the world that everything is possible by rising from the ashes and standing higher. She served as an example for the rest of the globe, in addition to herself. Instead of running from her concerns, she faced them head-on and overcame them. In the end, we all come to the realisation that success, wealth, and celebrity are not the sources of true pleasure. It can be found in thankfulness.

Muniba exclaimed, "I was so thrilled when I sat in a wheelchair for the first time." What if I didn't have legs? "I now have two wheels," she declared. Her life then abruptly turned around. Doctors urged her to keep pursuing her goals and passion, which was painting. Muniba quickly made a reputation for herself in the art world and demonstrated that a wheelchair is no barrier to success. She is presently regarded as one of Pakistan's top painters and artists. She uses oil pastels as her medium, and her company is called Muniba's Canvas, with the tagline "Let your walls wear colours."

Muniba is now a recipient of several honours and often delivers inspirational talks at conferences all over the world. She is a representative of Pakistan on the coveted Forbes 30 under 30 list of the world's best young leaders, entrepreneurs, and game-changers. Her additional accomplishments include serving as the Body Shop's brand ambassador; being Pond's miracle mentor; being Tony & Guy's wheelchair model; and being one of the BBC's 100 Most Inspirational Women of 2015. Additionally, chosen as a U.N. goodwill ambassador in Pakistan, Muniba is promoting women's empowerment there. Many people find inspiration in her life story, and she also conducts several TED presentations.

## *Believe in yourself; you are smarter than you believe you are.*

People hide their disabilities so often. They attempt to hide it because they believe that being disabled is neither attractive nor seductive. However, it is not the case. You are not impaired just because you have a disability. It enlightens you. You get knowledge from it. You learn something from it that someone without it will never understand. Many people believe that a model girl who is six feet tall and weighs 100 pounds (1.8 metres, 45 kg) represents perfection. I have no idea what part of the world you reside in, but I seldom see girls like that on the streets. I do see individuals with impairments and differences, and I believe that is what we need to portray as being authentic and beautiful, despite what people may view as flaws.

Everyone is entitled to the freedom to visit a restaurant. Everyone is entitled to the freedom to go on a date. Everyone is entitled to a chance and the right to employment. These goods, however, are not available to those with impairments.

Identity, significance, and perspective are the three dynamics that I name as being crucial to winning the war of the You-Factor. Knowing who you are and having a solid understanding of who you are establishes your identity. When you recognise your importance, you may realise the value and brilliance for which you were made. And if you grasp the concept of perspective, you may see your difficulties not as obstacles to success but as steppingstones to greatness. If you fully comprehend these three dynamics, you can control your You-Factor.

Healthy self-belief is neither arrogance, boasting, nor narcissism. Instead, it is a realistic yet upbeat assessment of who you are and what you are capable of. You are inspired to undertake things that you previously believed were impossible for you when you believe in yourself. You can take the first step, the next one, and then another step because of your faith. Before you know it, you're walking briskly along the road that once gave you anxiety.

*"With each encounter, when we truly pause to confront fear, we acquire strength, bravery, and confidence." We need to take action on what we believe we cannot. "*
*-Eleanor Roosevelt*

When you have self-belief, no setback or failure can make you lose confidence or cast doubt on your abilities. You won't always succeed despite your best efforts; you'll make errors like everyone else and make blunders, miss opportunities, and perform poorly. But there is a distinction. Your confidence gives you power.

You have to do it, and Roger Bannister is an example of this. He achieved the unthinkable and broke the "Four minute" barrier because he was absolutely positive that he would succeed, not simply because he thought he could. Many thousands of attempts ended in failure. Both physicians and scientists concurred that it couldn't be done. Not only was it risky, but it was also impossible. "Anyone who tried to run a mile in under four minutes would perish in an idiotic endeavour." He had an incorrect bone structure, too much wind resistance, insufficient lung capacity, and a heart that could not withstand the effort.

*"However ordinary each of us may seem, we are all in some way special, and can do things that are extraordinary, perhaps until then...even thought impossible." -Sir Roger Bannister*

People have been attempting to break the 4-minute barrier for years and years. Some came very, very close, but the record remained at 4:01.30 for about nine years as runners began to believe that perhaps, just perhaps, the experts were correct. Perhaps the human body had reached its limit, making it impossible. Then, on May 6, 1954, a chilly and rainy day in Oxford, England, a man by the name of Roger Bannister appeared to alter everything when, at the age of 25, he accomplished the unimaginable and ran the distance in 3:59.4. Everything that had previously been thought to be impossible became suddenly possible, and all preconceived notions that it couldn't be done were disproved.

*Whatever angle you choose, they all agree that hard work is the secret to real success.*

In reality, he often imagined achieving the goal as part of his training to instil confidence in his mind and body. Before actually breaking the record, he had experienced what it was like to do so. Without seeing any tangible evidence that it was possible, he was the only one who could generate assurance inside himself.

**"Every morning in Africa, a gazelle wakes up. It knows it must move faster than the lion or it will not survive. Every morning, a lion wakes up knowing it must move faster than the slowest gazelle or it will starve. It doesn't matter if you are the lion or the gazelle, when the sun comes up, you better be moving." -Roger Bannister**

Even more astounding than Bannister's inconceivable, world-record-breaking run is the fact that another runner achieved the same feat just 46 days later. And this time, he sprinted the distance in only 3.57.9 seconds, a whole 1.5 seconds quicker. Yes, another runner achieved the impossible not much longer than six weeks after Bannister.

However, as more and more athletes came to believe that it was feasible, more and more of them smashed the mark. By the end of 1957, almost three years after Bannister's unbelievable, record-breaking run, 16 athletes had also done the unthinkable and broken the four-minute barrier.How on earth is it even possible? How is it possible that other runners started to break the four-minute barrier so soon after Bannister did? Has human evolution had a rapid upswing? Did every runner suddenly start to improve? Did everyone alter their exercise and nutrition at the same time? Or was there another factor at play—something deeper?

You see, all it took was one man with a notion so deeply embedded in his head to challenge experts in his field and accomplish the seemingly impossible. You must act when you have such a strong belief in something and such a clear picture of it in your mind that it becomes your reality. Whatever it is, I don't care.

Roger Bannister is such a light and an example of mankind because of this. Not just because he was a fast runner or ran a mile in under four minutes, but also because he demonstrated to us that the only limitations we face are those that we place on ourselves. He accomplished the inconceivable, the unthinkable, and what both science and medical professionals believed could not be done.

*"Believe in yourself! Have faith in your abilities! Without a humble but reasonable confidence in your own powers you cannot be successful or happy."-Norman Vincent Peale*

It doesn't matter if you start off with skill, knowledge, or competence. Self-belief is the first step toward success. You start on a good note and give yourself a head start when you have a strong sense of self-belief.

Self-belief believes that you will succeed even before you start. You carry out all the actions of a champion because you behave and think like a successful person. As a result, your success starts to materialise because success becomes a skill that feeds itself.

Arunima Sinha has received several honours for her courageous example. She was involved in a railway accident in 2011 and lost her left leg as a result of a fight with robbers. Arunima was unfazed by the conditions as she used her prosthetic leg to ascend Mount Everest.

The first amputee from India to climb Mount Everest is Arunima Sinha. When she encountered a catastrophe on the train, it was reported by the media that she attempted suicide by jumping off the train. Later, her mother rectified the statement and clarified the situation with the media. Patients who have lost their legs often require 4 to 5 months to learn to walk again. Arunima Sinha, however, walked for two days. She did that because of her courage and drive. She raised the Indian flag for photos at the peak of Mount Everest. When she was taking photographs, she had less oxygen available. When the opportunity to quit shooting pictures presented itself, she decided to do so anyhow, even if it meant risking her life. Due to a lack of oxygen, Arunima Sinha believed she would not make it to sea level. But it just so happened that she ran upon a British climber who had turned back in the middle of their ascent. He provided her with oxygen, which let her survive until she returned to the camp.

Arunima Sinha is a role model for young people, demonstrating her determination to pursue her dream of proving herself to the world. In 2015, the President gave her "The Padma Shri," the fourth-highest civilian honour. She also discussed the "Ted Talk" platform, which broadcast her success and motivated young people all over the world.

*"By conquering all the seven summits I will prove that physical disability can never be a hindrance in achieving your life's goal if you have mental strength, strong willpower and firm determination."- Arunima Sinha*

Our culture is exceedingly materialistic. It quickly forms a shallow opinion of a person based just on how they seem physically. Society does nothing to assist those in need; it doesn't accept those who are different in terms of how they appear, move, or even speak, and believes that they are superior to those who are disabled. But throughout history, several individuals have demonstrated that their physical limitations could not overcome their strong will, and in this article, we will learn about a few of those motivational figures.

*"No matter how great a loss, time always heals the pain, even though the scars remain. Sometimes when you help someone else, you also end up helping yourself"-Arunima Sinha*

Never let anyone tell you what you can or cannot do. Don't allow other people's limitations to restrict your vision. You will find a way if you don't give up on something you genuinely believe in.

You can do things you never imagined possible if you can get rid of your self-doubt and have faith in yourself. What is the relationship between accomplishment and self-belief? Self-belief is the foundation upon which you can build the life of your dreams. Your protection against the what-if scenario that occasionally enters your mind is self-belief. Self-belief keeps you going when you are aware that the deck is stacked against you, your opponent is stronger than you, and everyone believes that you can't compete with him.

*No one is born with all the skills, abilities, or information; everyone learns in their areas of passion.*

The inner voice encourages you to follow your gut, rise to the occasion, and take measured risks. By doing so, you may expand your horizons and empower yourself to achieve greater things. High self-esteem and a feeling of self are characteristics of those who believe in themselves. They have unconditional love and acceptance for themselves and don't care what people think or say about them. Their own opinions are the only ones that matter to them.

All of your self-doubts, anxieties, and apprehensions are dispelled by self-belief. People with conviction are motivated from the inside out and exert great effort to achieve their objectives. Only when you have a strong belief from the inside out can you overcome obstacles and give every task you take on your best effort. When you decide to seek achievement, you will frequently face hardships and challenges. However, having confidence in yourself will give you the strength to act with unwavering dedication to your objective.

*We become more receptive to the beneficial impacts that good emotions have on our resilience and overall well-being when we include more love, kindness, empathy, and compassion into our lives.*

When you have confidence, you understand that you alone are accountable for your achievements and that, with enough willpower, you can accomplish everything you set your mind to. There is an abundance of information available, and there are no restrictions on the knowledge or skills you may pick up. The convenience of having everything at our fingertips in the digital era is a gift. All you need is an eagerness to learn and an open mind. When you have self-belief, no setback or failure can make you lose confidence or cast doubt on your abilities. You won't always succeed despite your best efforts; you'll make errors like everyone else and make blunders, miss opportunities, and perform poorly. But there is a distinction. Your confidence gives you power.

Positive feelings are highly regarded and actively sought after. Positive feelings, however, may have long-term advantages in significant areas, such as jobs, physical health, and interpersonal relationships, beyond simply being enjoyable. The focus of research so far has been on the more general purposes of happy emotions. The broaden-and-build hypothesis holds that people may develop their social, psychological, and intellectual capabilities by expanding their thought-action repertoires in response to pleasant feelings.

*"The best and most beautiful things in the world cannot be seen or even touched. They must be felt with the heart."*
*– Helen Keller*

According to recent research, people may be motivated to participate in constructive activities that will better themselves by experiencing happy feelings, especially thankfulness. We suggest and provide evidence for the idea that being grateful motivates people to make an attempt to better themselves through increasing connectivity, elevation, humility, and some negative feelings like indebtedness. Social media represents the carefully curated lifestyles we want the world to see. Due to the fact that social media is now carefully curated to reflect the lifestyles we want others to see us leading, it often provides an inaccurate reflection of how individuals actually live. As we anxiously compare our social media clout based on the number of followers we have, there is pressure to provide the most "likeable" material. We now have a superpower thanks to social media, but we might not have been utilising it properly.

*"Emotion is more powerful than reason. Emotion is the driving force behind thinking and reasoning. Emotional intelligence increases the mind's ability to make positive, brilliant decisions." – Dr. T.P. Chia*

Thanks to the digital world, we can communicate with almost everyone on the planet in real time. It enables us to stay in touch with far-off relatives and friends. It enables us to openly share our ideas with the world so that they might be seen and perhaps benefited from. But we frequently use it for slander, harassment, and trolling. It serves as a place for us to express our emotional suffering. We use it to quarrel and fight with people over unimportant issues.

*"The only thing that stands between you and your wellbeing is a simple fact: you have allowed your thoughts and emotions to take instruction from the outside rather than within."- Sadguru*

So now consider this: What if every word, social media post, email, and uploaded image were to remain there indefinitely? A digital trail that determines how others will remember you? In your current form, would you still utilise social media? Most likely not. Would your opinion change if there was no visible display of likes and followers? Does our lust for social currency alter who we are at our core? You might not think that being emotionally aware has much to do with business.

*"Don't shut down your emotions. Embrace them. Your emotions are your internal compass telling you whether or not you are on track. Use them to help cultivate your passions or motivate you to change situations and circumstances that hold you back from achieving your goals." – Jillian Michaels*

Nevertheless, several studies have indicated that unfavourable work environments might affect the well-being of families that have employees as members. In other words, employees bring the stress and hostility they experience at work into their personal lives and relationships. According to a recent Harvard Business Review article, the effect was that the stress people face at work crosses over to and hinders the functioning and well-being of family members, including harming children's academic achievement.

*"We can never obtain peace in the outer world until we make peace with ourselves." -Dalai Lama*

Negative emotion storage is detrimental to your health. It will ultimately find a way out, and a sympathetic ear is the best place for it. Keeping difficulties to oneself can result in a variety of physical and mental stress, including headaches, stomach cramps, and restlessness, without you even realising it. Speak to someone, whether a friend or a professional, if you're feeling overwhelmed and in need of assistance. They could provide you with the suggestions or guidance you need.

Are you leading the best life you can? You are not living life to the fullest if you answered "no," "I'm not sure," or "maybe" to the question above. This truly shouldn't be the case considering that you are in charge of creating your own life experience. Everyone has good and bad days, but the most important thing is to make the most of each day, regardless of how it goes. Be prepared to fail.

*The more mistakes you make and the more experience you have, the higher your chances of success.*

You may occasionally feel anxious, concerned, in pain, or utterly bored and try to hide this truth. Take control of your emotions by noticing when you experience odd highs or lows and considering why. List the events from the previous week that gave you energy and made you feel down on paper. You may create such a list each week and take one step away from "depressors" and toward "energizers." This will gradually liberate your potential. However, there are numerous personality tests that are available that may help you identify your inherent traits and talents. Observing your feelings is a terrific way to appreciate your individuality and potential. Attempt the Strengthsfinder, Myers-Briggs, Enneagram, or other assessment.

*"Ordinary people think merely of spending time, great people think of using it." -Arthur Schopenhauer*

Take careful note of the lessons you may use from each incident if you want to get better. Be ready to be let down. Many people go to great lengths to avoid being let down. They learn to negatively connect with disappointment. However, disappointment is a normal aspect of being human since it reveals your actual emotions. Instead of resisting it, accept it. Learn to control your emotions and unhappiness to achieve more in life. I believe that living is a beautiful experience.

*"Thoughts and emotions come from the same source. Thoughts are the dry expressions of the mind, emotions are juicy. The way you think is the way you feel."- Sadguru*

*You must move from rejection to transformation to leave a legacy.*

When we get into the idea that "I think, therefore I am," we become unable to separate ourselves from our ideas. Your thoughts are not all that you are. They are not the reason you suffer or are unhappy; instead, you suffer because you connect with them and get attached to them. When we think that our thoughts are reality, chaos results.

*"No one cares how much you know, until they know how much you care." -Theodore Roosevelt*

People act out their thoughts in troubled parts of the world, which causes issues. We don't need to participate in peace marches or protests to achieve peace; it is much easier than that. It starts with our ideas and spreads across our lives and those of others. The matter is how justifiable our cause, when we hold onto our ideas with hostility, violence, and suffering spread over the globe. Peace is fostered through practising non-aggression. Think about an unkind thought you could have about someone else. If it is given too much attention, it agitates other ideas and produces undesirable results.

*"It's not that I'm so smart, it's just that I stay with problems longer."-Albert Einstein*

Steve Jobs is credited for helping Apple grow into the world's largest corporation. However, it is really astonishing to learn that the multi-billion dollars firm, which currently employs over 130 thousand people, was first founded by just two people in a garage. Additionally, it should be noted that this outstanding entrepreneur was sacked and let go from the business where he first began his career. In addition, after discovering his potential and talents, Steve Jobs moved forward with the creation of the largest firm in the world, known as "Apple."

*"When dealing with people, remember you are not dealing with creatures of logic, but with creatures of emotion." -Dale Carnegie*

It was considerably more crucial for Bill Gates to learn from failure than it was to rejoice in victory. This brilliant businessman, a Harvard dropout, is responsible for making Microsoft the largest software corporation. In addition, he was well-known for the greatest business failure in history, Traf-O-Data, a self-owned company entity. Bill Gates' whole investment was lost, and regrettably, even the education could not be finished. But his intense drive and enthusiasm for everything related to computer programming inspired him to start the world's largest software firm under the trade name "Microsoft."

*"Many of life's failures are people who did not realize how close they were to success when they gave up."-Thomas Edison*

The inventor of the delicious milk-chocolate delight we all adore, Milton Hershey, wasn't immediately successful. He had previously worked at a nearby candy manufacturer before starting his own candy company. But when he made the decision to go out on his own, he utterly failed. Despite suffering two more setbacks, he went back to the family farm and mastered the technique of producing beautiful milk chocolate candies, which we now enjoy in the form of Hershey's chocolate.

*"Failure is only the opportunity to begin again, this time more intelligently."-Henry Ford*

Walt Disney's first job was getting sacked by a newspaper because he wasn't innovative enough. Later, since they were thought to be "too disturbing for women," his Mickey Mouse cartoons were rejected. The fact that "The Three Little Pigs" only had four characters added insult to injury. The majority of the time, we tend to blame fate for our failure. The number of rejections you experience is typically inversely correlated with your level of success.

The enemies of success are rejection and anxiety. If you postpone making difficult calls out of concern that others may reject you (such as clients, workers, coworkers, or colleagues), your effectiveness will suffer. But overcoming that fear is just the beginning. If you truly want to succeed, you must figure out how to use rejection as a tool to propel you closer to your long-term objectives.

*"We all learn lessons in life. Some stick, some don't. I have always learned more from rejection and failure than from acceptance and success." – Henry Rollins*

Imagine you get the opportunity to present your elevator pitch to a significant investor. Despite your best efforts, the investor just tells you to "go away" or, worse yet, "your concept stinks; we'll contact you." If you were hoping to get any investment capital, it is undoubtedly a dismal result. But why would you feel "rejected" as opposed to, say, annoyed, irate, or sad? The reason is that, rather than focusing on the problem itself, you took the investor's remarks personally and allowed them to make you feel horrible about yourself.

*"You only have to do a very few things right in your life so long as you don't do too many things wrong." --Warren Buffett*

If you feel like you are receiving too many rejections, examine the expectations of other individuals who are doing what you are. Salespeople, for example, may make 100 calls before identifying a prospect; similarly, entrepreneurs may give presentations to dozens of investors before receiving financing. If you are emotionally invested in the other person, disassociate yourself from the result of the scenario. Even if the prospect you've been courting for months doesn't end up buying, you've still created a wonderful business connection.

*"I hated every minute of training, but I said, 'Don't quit. Suffer now and live the rest of your life as a champion." –*
*Muhammad Ali*

If you believe the other person to be extremely significant, balance your appreciation with a healthy dose of realism. Even well-known business moguls are often below-average performers who luck into success. Even if not, they are still just regular individuals like you and me and not gods on earth. After gaining some perspective on your feelings, it's important to use some practical reasoning to distinguish between legitimate and unjustified complaints.

*"I take rejection as someone blowing a bugle in my ear to wake me up and get going, rather than retreat." –*
*Sylvester Stallone*

When a person refuses to do what you ask them to because of anything within your control, this is a justified refusal. When your "failure" occurred as a result of an arbitrary event outside of your control, that rejection is illegitimate. Consider the scenario when you meet with a client and say something foolish, like the wrong client's name. The customer's departure is a legitimate rejection because you were to blame for the triggering event. Success isn't always more than a numbers game.

*"Your work is going to fill a large part of your life, and the only way to be truly satisfied is to do what you believe is great work. And the only way to do great work is to love what you do. If you haven't found it yet, keep looking. Don't settle. As with all matters of the heart, you'll know when you find it." -Steve Jobs*

I sent the concept for my first business book to a lot of editors and received a lot of "rejection letters." Instead of giving up, I began each day by spreading the letters out on the ground and using them as stepping stones. A lot of individuals are stopped in their tracks by the pain of rejection. In an effort to reduce the possibility of more rejections, they started acting cautiously. But psychologically powerful individuals don't behave that way. Whether they were rejected by a potential love partner or passed over for a promotion, they bounce back stronger than before.

> *"It is during our darkest moments that we must focus to see the light." – Aristotle*

You could feel better for a moment by putting on a brave front and saying things like, "I didn't want that job anyhow." However, attempting to make yourself—or people around you—believe that you don't care won't help you in the long run to mend your injured ego. When someone is mentally strong, they will disclose when they are truly ashamed, wounded, or dissatisfied. By confronting their feelings, they can recover from their suffering in a healthy way.

> *"If you aren't getting rejected on a daily basis, your goals aren't ambitious enough."-Chris Dixon*

It might be easy to exaggerate your bad luck or make dire predictions about how a single rejection would cause you to live in sorrow for the rest of your life. You'll remain trapped if you think statements like "I'll never move up the corporate ladder" or "No one will ever believe in me." People with strong minds won't have a sad party. Instead, they tell themselves that being rejected isn't the end of the world and they create a strategy for moving on. You probably aren't trying to reach your full potential if you aren't getting rejected.

Rejection is evidence that you stretched yourself and sought to widen your horizons. People with strong mental faculties are proud of themselves for being ready to push themselves. They understand that being declined or passed over demonstrates that they are truly enjoying life to the fullest.

*Rejection is a hard emotion to deal with and an even harder message to hear. When we are faced with rejection, it can be a hit to our ego, or it can make us question if we are good enough.*

If an employer rejects your application, you could assume that you are totally unqualified. Or, you can conclude you're ugly if a partner rejects you. However, making broad generalisations based on one person's viewpoint will only make you slower. People with good mental faculties don't let other people's opinions determine their sense of value. Instead, despite being rejected, they are aware of who they are and what they are capable of. It might be tempting to listen to your inner critic when you're feeling bad. But telling yourself you're a failure or that you'll never be successful will simply make rejection hurt worse.

*Sometimes what we learn from rejection, ends up ultimately making us the best version of ourselves, and in the best possible position.*

People with high mental faculties are kind to themselves. They don't criticise themselves for their shortcomings and speak to themselves like a valued friend might. They heal more quickly and efficiently thanks to their positive self-talk. If you're willing to learn, rejection may be a useful instructor. You won't become better by criticising yourself, coming up with reasons why you failed, or placing blame on others.

People with high mental faculties not only put up with discomfort, but also use it as a teaching opportunity. They constantly reflect on what they have learned. They get more aware and more determined with each rejection they receive. If you're not careful, rejection may halt you in your tracks. However, assuming you're "out of your league" will restrict your possibilities. Mentally tough individuals allow themselves time to heal after a particularly traumatic rejection. They search for other possibilities once they're prepared.

*"Life is 10% what happens to you and 90% how you react to it."- Charles R. Swindoll*

Success constantly puts itself forward rather than the made-up myths and looks past the ridiculous justifications. Success is the outcome of strong perseverance and attention when going forward along the working road.

*"A failure is not always a mistake. It may simply be the best one can do under the circumstances. The real mistake is to stop trying." -B.F. Skinner*

## You can leave a legacy because you control your destiny.

You are in charge of your own destiny. You have undoubtedly heard this a lot in your life. Maybe this resonates with you, or maybe you feel that the sentiment condescendingly oversimplifies the difficulties of life that might restrict your alternatives. Whether or not you feel like you have complete control over your destiny, the truth is that you do. Controlling your ideas is a key component in shaping (or influencing) your future. The viewpoint that you have influence over what happens rather than feeling as though something is happening to you is created by viewing problems as opportunities. Because of this, you may take action and affect change as opposed to just accepting your circumstances.

*"Experience is not what happens to you--it's how you interpret what happens to you." -Aldous Huxley*

You ought to take into account how you view yourself. Remind yourself that you are never a passive victim of your circumstances since pride is something to exercise. You have the power to control your circumstances and alter your course.

*"Control your own destiny or someone else will."-Jack Welch*

A life with meaning is abundant when you operate from the level of the soul. Please bear with me as we go a little deeper into this. Living from the soul level entails letting go of our ideas about how life ought to be. You have a more profound understanding of your spiritual existence. It necessitates focusing on your actual essence, independent of your worldview. These are ideas you developed to help you make sense of your surroundings, but they serve no more purpose than a motorcycle's training wheels.

*"You are the master of your destiny. You can influence, direct and control your own environment. You can make your life what you want it to be."-Napoleon Hill*

When things do not go as planned or as we had hoped, we frequently blame it on fate. The opposite is also true in that some individuals frequently blame others' success on their fate rather than recognising the effort they put into their accomplishments. In other words, we associate our choices with our future.

*"It's not whether the glass is half empty or half full, it's who is pouring the water. The key in business and success at any endeavor is doing your best to control your destiny. You can't always do it, but you have to take every opportunity you can to be as prepared as-and ahead of-the competition as you possibly can be."-Mark Cuban*

We frequently believe that destiny, a great power, governs our lives rather than ourselves. What one should understand, though, is that a man's fate is determined by his mind and the thoughts he puts into action. Thank goodness Walt decided to ignore all of his detractors and pursue his ambitions instead of listening to them, as a result of which we now have the Disney corporation.

*"All success in life, whether material or spiritual, starts with the thoughts that you put into your mind every second of every minute of every day. Your outer world reflects the state of your inner world. By controlling the thoughts that you think and the way you respond to the events of your life, you begin to control your destiny."-Rohit Sharma*

A determined intellect might lead you to destinations you never imagined. That is why the phrase "It's all in the head" is so popular. Only the choices we make will determine our future.

Successful individuals handle situations differently. They just alter their reactions to the occurrences until they get the desired results. You have the power to alter your behaviour, communication style, mental representations of the world, and way of thinking (the things you do). You essentially just have control over it. Unfortunately, the majority of us are controlled by our routines. We become mired in conditioned reactions to our partners and kids, our coworkers, our clients and customers, our students, and the rest of the world.

*"Your destiny is to fulfill those things upon which you focus most intently. So choose to keep your focus on that which is truly magnificent, beautiful, uplifting and joyful. Your life is always moving toward something."-Ralph Marston*

You must learn to regulate your ideas, pictures, dreams, daydreams, and actions. Your thoughts, words, and actions must all be deliberate and in line with your mission, beliefs, and objectives. Sometimes you come up with a brilliant concept right away that you can develop and run with. Everything seems to be going great until you have a setback. You get punched in the gut by failure, leaving you with aching wounds and no choice but to whine about what might have been. Change your replies if you don't like the results.

*"The law of harvest is to reap more than you sow. Sow an act, and you reap a habit. Sow a habit and you reap a character. Sow a character and you reap a destiny."- James Allen*

Our ideas are the embodiment of our minds, and our actions are the result of those thoughts. One just cannot sit back, fold his arms, and claim that everything in his or her life is the result of fate. Our way of thinking and the way we see the world directly affect how we live. Only the choices we make will determine our future. For instance, if a person has a strong will and a determined attitude, the decision-making process and how the choice is carried out will eventually establish that person's fate, which will finally determine their destiny.

*"Life is not always going to be roses and rainbows. You are going to have uncomfortable moments. It's what we do with those moments that is going to count and determine our destiny."-Lana*

We are solely responsible for our own destinies. Whether things turn out better or worse depends entirely on how we perceive and respond to the events that occur in our lives. One's fate is decided by the way they think and behave. Our thoughts have a major role in how we behave, and our actions play a major role in how we are seen by others. Therefore, a man with control over his thoughts has power over his actions, which in turn gives him control over any circumstances in life that may eventually determine his fate.

*"Your destiny is to fulfill those things upon which you focus most intently. So choose to keep your focus on that which is truly magnificent, beautiful, uplifting and joyful. Your life is always moving toward something."-Ralph Marston*

Considering that everything is temporary, try to avoid being attached to people, places, or events. Dread is the source of clinging, which breeds more fear. Change your thoughts to more powerful ones so that you can easily allow what is required to flow into your experience. Don't hold onto things you don't need anymore. Consider repurposing it if you haven't used it in the past three months. Less tangible possessions free us from having to handle more. I'm not advocating leading a simple existence; rather, you shouldn't look to worldly items to bolster your sense of identity.

*"The high destiny of the individual is to serve rather than to rule."-Albert Einstein*

Michael Joseph Jackson, better known as the "King of Pop," was a multi-talented musical performer who had great success both as a solo artist, best-selling American singer, songwriter, and dancer. MJ began his musical career at the young age of 5 with encouragement from his father, Joseph

Walter Jackson, and went on to become acknowledged as the greatest entertainer of the 20<sup>th</sup> century. He was in the spotlight for more than four decades thanks to his well-known moonwalk dancing style and fashion specialties like his crystal gloves and the 1980s trophy jacket trend that was immortalised. The second best-selling album in history, Thriller, included Jackson's most well-known work. He then went on to create a string of successful singles, including Bad, Dangerous, Off the Wall, History, and Invincible. Among his greatest accomplishments are 31 Guinness World Records, 13 Grammy Awards, 26 American Music Awards, five consecutive Billboard Top 10 singles, etc.

Whatever you choose to call it—destiny, fate, karma, serendipity—the notion that life is predetermined by forces outside of our control is an age-old one. It exists in every culture on earth, including ancient Chinese narrative and Greek mythology. But what if fate wasn't actually real? What if you had influence over your future?

*"Anything that happens in your life was meant to happen. It is your destiny. I was destined to have the life I have now, and I can't have any regrets."- Zlatan Ibrahimovic*

You have acknowledged your internal centre of control if you think you are in charge of your own destiny. It means that you accept responsibility for your thoughts, actions, and results. This method of thinking can help you become unstoppable. You may learn to take charge of your future. You must first embrace who you are and where you are right now in order to take control of your future. You'll run out of things to do if you trick yourself into thinking that you're further along in your goals than you actually are.

*"Your life will be no better than the plans you make and the action you take. You are the architect and builder of your own life, fortune, destiny."- Alfred A. Montapert*

Don't delude yourself into thinking your life is worse than it is, though. Take a step back and consider your situation differently. Increase your awareness of yourself and embrace the truth. If you don't know where you're starting from, you can't develop a strategy to control your fate. Accepting reality does not entail passively accepting your fate without taking any action. It entails taking responsibility for the things you can alter and letting go of the things you can't. You have no influence over what people believe or do. You have no power over the market. Your own mentality is the only thing you have control over. To do that, you must challenge the self-talk you believe in and replace it with an empowering one.

*"The torment of precautions often exceeds the dangers to be avoided. It is sometimes better to abandon one's self to destiny."- Napoleon Bonaparte*

Because of the level of brilliance he showed in his work, he is regarded as one of the greatest individuals in the world, and others enrol in music production classes in an effort to emulate him. All of us who live in this beautiful world aspire to success.

*"We need a spirit of victory, a spirit that will carry us to our rightful place under the sun, a spirit which can recognize that we, as inheritors of a proud civilization, are entitled to our rightful place on this planet. If that indomitable spirit were to arise, nothing can hold us from achieving our rightful destiny."- C. V. Raman*

We all have the innate drive to succeed and move steadily in the direction of greater success, regardless of whether the person in question is a kid, a young adult, or an elderly person. Any location, including schools, universities, coaching, professional settings such as companies, workplaces, etc., to name a few, may usually exhibit a competitive mindset.

When compared to the effort we put into achieving success, we frequently have higher expectations and hope that it will arrive sooner rather than later. If it does not, we tend to become upset and eventually sink farther into the pit of inferiority. The majority of individuals have observed this circumstance, when regular and committed efforts are neglected and only failures are celebrated. Such instances may be found anywhere in the world. The majority of famous people have had significant setbacks in their battles with life. Nevertheless, they persisted in their paths to success and eventually experienced enormous success in their specialised industries. They never let their race, religion, or any other distinction stand in the way of their achievement.

*Choosing your new way of life when do we truly stop and realise that our behaviours are harming us? How do you go about developing healthy habits and a new way of life?*

On the basis of events and observations from previous lives, one's conception of man may alter. Your thoughts will get better as you watch and learn more, which will improve how you think and behave. Successful individuals spend a lot of time considering what and how they should act, and it is this way of thinking that has enabled them to change their fate and achieve better things in life. A strong and capable intellect is capable of great things. A man's ability to regulate his thoughts and use willpower is what enables him to achieve so much in life. The mindset that "it was destined to be" brings about disaster because it causes us to give up on our efforts to continuously work toward success and instead to use this as a justification for our failures.

*"Every individual soul chooses the significant people in that life. Destiny will place you in the particular circumstance; it will dictate that you will encounter a particular person, at a certain time, place."- Brian Weiss*

Therefore, we should alter our perspectives and behaviour and continue to make attempts and endeavour in the quest for our achievement, which will define our fate. We can absolutely change our fate if we can change our minds. In our hands, it is. Just three years before the release of the first Harry Potter novel, Harry Potter and The Philosopher's Stone, in 1994, J.K. Rowling had recently gone through a divorce, was receiving government assistance, and could barely afford to feed her infant. She had to physically type each version to send to publishers since she could not afford a computer or even the expense of photocopying the 90,000-word novel at the time she was shopping it around. It was repeatedly turned down until a tiny London publisher named Bloomsbury decided to resubmit it after the CEO's eight-year-old daughter fell in love with it.

*"I believe that you control your destiny, that you can be what you want to be. You can also stop and say, 'No, I won't do it, I won't behave this way anymore. I'm lonely and I need people around me, maybe I have to change my methods of behaving,' and then you do it."-Leo Buscaglia*

As you overcome challenges and correct errors, you will amass evidence that you are a strong woman, evidence that you can draw on when you begin to doubt your abilities. You always have a choice in how you react to the things that life throws your way, whether they are good or negative. You can choose to run away from a difficulty, let it overtake you, or make an effort to conquer it. Although none of these choices will always be the ideal ones for you in the long term, strive to be aware of your possibilities.

*"As long as we are persistence in our pursuit of our deepest destiny, we will continue to grow. We cannot choose the day or time when we will fully bloom. It happens in its own time."-Denis Waitley*

Occasionally, despite your greatest efforts, you will fall short. You could fail at social contact, be unable to rescue a dying relationship, or fail to accomplish a goal. These things have the power to make you feel bad about yourself and set you back considerably. When anything goes wrong, take a time to gather your thoughts before deciding whether to try again. Perhaps you can mend the bond or begin a new one with someone else. You can apologise for making a social faux pas and elaborate on your intentions.

*"You are the creator of your destiny." -Swami Vivekanand*

Sometimes, falling short of your goals might even be beneficial. Being knocked down may ignite a fire within you that motivates you to succeed. You can always learn from your failures, so take the time to reflect on what went wrong in your last attempt and make plans on how to improve going forward.

*"You can't connect the dots looking forward; you can only connect them looking backward. So you have to trust that the dots will somehow connect in your future. You have to trust in something – your gut, destiny, life, karma, whatever. This approach has never let me down, and it has made all the difference in my life. "-Steve Jobs*

You will learn new things about yourself, the best ways for you to work, and the greatest strategies to get things done. Other times, failure may help you gain perspective and see that what you were doing wasn't feasible or appropriate for you. There are numerous ways forward; pick one that appeals to you and makes you optimistic about the future. You will increase your personal confidence while boosting other people's confidence in you. They will be impressed by your grace when they see how you face problems head-on and get through barriers in life.

*"If you believe in destiny, then you know that you have a purpose. You know things happen for a reason, and that you should find out how to live up to that essence of what you're supposed to do and which direction you are determined to take."- V. Noot*

When others respect you, you will be exposed to more possibilities and have the freedom to select which ones you want to pursue. All of a sudden, you're back in charge! Keep in mind the things you can manage when life seems out of control and you lack agency. A shift in perspective might set off a chain of events that will transform you into the master of your own destiny.

Many people make unwise judgments in the haste of life and abuse alcohol or drugs. Many other people struggle with sadness or anxiety. We experience a crisis—a collapse on the physical, emotional, or spiritual levels—when life goes on uncontrolled. Recovery depends on both physical and mental wellbeing. Creating healthy behaviours and drawing on spiritual inspiration. The incredible power of inspiration examines the tale of our lives first from the outside in, starting with our circumstances and ending with our feelings, and then from the inside out, starting with our dreams and ending with the outer world. This ground-breaking holistic approach to the body, mind, and spirit enables readers to break bad habits and create healthier, more fulfilling lives.

*"Destiny is a name often given in retrospect to choices that had dramatic consequences."- J.K. Rowling*

Limiting beliefs, or the unfavourable things we tell ourselves about who we are and how the world operates, only prevent you from having complete control over your future. The motivation behind your actions, or your driving force, may also be gleaned from your connections. Six human needs—certainty, importance, diversity, love/connection, development, and contribution—are what motivate each of us. We all require these things on some level, but each of us has a primary need that dominates all others.

You'll be able to better manage your destiny if you see your life in this light, since you'll be able to identify and meet your needs in healthy ways. Although it is a survival mechanism, fear doesn't always help us, just like in relationships. Living in fear prevents you from ever learning how to master your destiny.

*You may effectively realise your full potential, change the narrative, and adopt a new way of life. With the help of this potent technique, you may become your own hero, rewrite your own stories, and empower yourselves to lead fulfilling lives.*

You must learn to control your fear rather than allow it to control you if you want to reach your full potential and become the best version of yourself. Be open and honest with your spouse. Take action to launch the company you've always wanted. Enroll in a public speaking course. Do whatever it is you're terrified of right now.

*Go beyond the limitations you unconsciously create for yourselves, and live your life to the fullest. If you shift from unwillingness to willingness, from inertia to effervescence, your life will become joyful; your journey will become effortless.*

# About The Author

*Dr. Amit Das, is a renowned executive advisor, consultant, educationist, author, speaker, counsellor, and coach whose 25+ years of business experience provides high-impact, practical solutions that support his clients' leadership development and organisational transformations. He worked for fortune 500 companies and left rich leagacy of organising transformational learning workshops. He has transformed more than 5000+ working executives through his path breaking capability building learning workshops. Dr. Amit Das is recognised as an innovative, principled thought leader who combines intellectual rigor and discipline with an ability to translate theory into practice. His operational skills are coupled with a strategic ability to analyse, develop, and implement successful strategies for profitability, growth, and sustainability.*

*Dr. Amit Das has a successful track record in aligning learning and training solutions to key business strategy with a strong focus on flawless execution excellence to facilitate individual, business divisional, and organisational performance. He keeps relentless focus on measuring training impact and ROI, people capability building graphs, training process governance, performance coaching, and strategic thinking. These have been some of his key individual success traits. His core capabilities include performance coaching, designing training and development frameworks, psychometric assessment and analysis, competency framework development and assessments, content design and facilitation of soft skills and leadership programmes, Learning Management Systems, Learning Impact Measurement, Talent Analysis, and Performance Coaching and Counselling.*

*Dr. Amit Das has authored multiple management and self-development books, like The Alchemy Of Resilient Leadership, Redefining Organisational Excellence, High Impact Leadership, Redefining Corporate Spectrum, Create Your Leadership Edge, Love-Laugh- Live With Happiness, SMART Parenting @ Zero Cost, Redefining HRM, Building Organisational Capability, Ethical Road Map, Attomic Attention, BYPB, Redefining The Power Of Mentoring, Making The Most Future Fit Organisation, Redefining Talent Management, Defining Your Success Factors, Lead or Plead, Make The Most Of Your Life, Better Half or Bitter Half, Psychology Of Learning And Development, The Transformative Mind & Soul are few of them.*

*He has a Ph.D. and a Fellowship in strategic learning, along with his first class degrees in Human Resource Management, Marketing Management, International Business, and Corporate Laws from the top business schools in India. He is a certified Psychometric analyst, HR Analyst, OD Interventionist, Human Psychologist, Lifecoach, Leadership Developer, Black Belt (LSS), Strategic Thinker, Talent Analyst, certified professional trainer from the U.K. and certified behavioral coach from the U.S.A.*

*Dr. Amit Das likes googling, reading books, writing articles & books, cooking, listening to old melodies, and counselling people to unleash their true potential to build a strong nation. He is married and blessed with a son. He would love to hear about your experience after reading his books. You can email him and share your thoughts, or you can use his services for life coaching, positive behavioural counseling, educational support, and mentoring for young, promising students pursuing their B.B.A. and M.B.A. degrees.*

# References


- *Think and Grow Rich: The Landmark Bestseller Now Revised and Updated for the 21st Century (Think and Grow Rich Series), January, 2005 by Napoleon Hill , Arthur R. Pell.*
- *Now, Discover Your Strengths: The revolutionary Gallup program that shows you how to develop your unique talents and strengths, February, 2020 by Gallup.*
- *Change Your Life: End Your Struggle & Create an Extraordinary Life in 10 Days Paperback – 29 September 2019 by Sneh Desai (Author).*
- *Change Your Life In Seven Days: The No. 1 Bestseller Paperback – 30 May 2019 by Paul McKenna (Author).*
- *Change Your Brain, Change Your Life (Revised and Expanded) Paperback – 3 November 2015 by Daniel G. Amen M.D. (Author).*
- *Change your Habits, Change your Life Paperback – 1 January 2019 by Thomas C. Corley (Author).*
- *The Power of Positive Thinking, March, 2003 by Dr. Norman Vincent Peale.*
- *High-Hanging Fruit: Build Something Great by Going Where No One Else Will, July, 2016 by Mark Rampolla.*
- *Choose Yourself! June, 2013 by James Altucher, Dick Costolo.*
- *Mindset: The New Psychology of Success, December, 2007 by Carol S. Dweck.*
- *Man's Search for Meaning, June , 2006 by Viktor E. Frankl.*
- *You Are a Badass: How to Stop Doubting Your Greatness and Start Living an Awesome Life, April, 2013 by Jen Sincero.*

- *Make Your Bed: Little Things That Can Change Your Life...And Maybe the World*, April, 2017 by Admiral William H. McRaven.
- *The Alchemist, 25th Anniversary: A Fable About Following Your Dream*, April, 2014 by Paulo Coelho.
- *Smarter Faster Better: The Transformative Power of Real Productivity*, March, 2017 by Charles Duhigg.
- *Tuesdays with Morrie: An Old Man, a Young Man, and Life's Greatest Lesson, 25th Anniversary Edition Kindle Edition*, June, 2007 by Mitch Albom.
- *The 5 Second Rule: Transform your Life, Work, and Confidence with Everyday Courage*, February, 2017 by Mel Robbins.
- *Unfu*k Yourself: Get Out of Your Head and into Your Life*, August, 2017 by Gary John Bishop.
- *Hustle: The Power to Charge Your Life with Money, Meaning, and Momentum*, September, 2016 by Neil Patel, Patrick Vlaskovits, and Jonas Koffler.
- *Directed by Purpose: How to Focus on Work That Matters, Ignore Distractions and Manage Your Attention over the Long Haul (Six Simple Steps to Success Book 5) Kindle Edition*, July,2021 by Michal Stawicki , Anthony Smits.
- *Change Your Schedule, Change Your Life Paperback – 30 January 2018 by Suhas Kshirsagar (Author), Michelle D. Seaton (Author).*
- *Change Your Morning, Change Your Life: A step-by-step guide to developing life changing habits that will shape the future you want. Kindle Edition by Val Currey (Author), November, 2022.*
- *The 7 seconds that can change your life Perfect Paperback – 21 September 2022 by Imraana Varcie (Author).*
- *One Day, Life Will Change: A story of love and inspiration to win life when it hits you hard, Paperback – 1 March 2020*

*by Saranya Umakanthan (Author).*

- *The Positive Way To Change Your Life Paperback – 11 October 2012 by Norman Vincent Peale.*
- *The Happiness Tree: Grow Your Happiness by Cultivating a Healthy, Creative and Purposeful Life Paperback – December, 2015 by Shane Eric Mathias.*
- *Who Do You Want to Be? Paperback – May, 2021 by Alina Shahnazari.*
- *The Purpose Driven Life: What on Earth Am I Here For? Paperback –June 2016 by Rick Warren.*
- *Provisions For Your Purpose Kindle Edition, May,2022. by Adetola Balogun.*
- *Purposeful: A Step-by-Step Guide to Finding Clear Direction in a Chaotic World Paperback – September, 2016 by John Carroll.*
- *On Purpose: The Busy Woman's Guide to an Extraordinary Life of Meaning and Success Kindle Edition, October,2021 by Tanya Dalton.*
- *On Purposeful Systems: An Interdisciplinary Analysis of Individual and Social Behavior as a System of Purposeful Events Paperback –July, 2005 by Fred Emery.*
- *Living a Purposeful and Fruitful Life : The 33 Principles Kindle Edition,January,2021. by Michael O. A. Asenso , Nana Amma Oforiwaa Sam.*
- *Incredible Power of Inspiration: Creating the Life You Yearn for Paperback – October, 2017 by Jenifer Zetlan.*
- *Wise Mind Living: Master Your Emotions, Transform Your Life Paperback –January, 2017 by Erin Olivo Ph.D.*
- *Finding Purpose Beyond Oneself: How to Live a Fulfilling Life & Find Your Life's Work by Focusing on Others Instead of Yourself (15 Minute Life Series Book 1) Kindle Edition by Sean Bobby Maximilian, Nov, 2016.*
- *Finding Your Purpose: How to Find Your Purpose In Life*

and Make the Most of Your Time Here on Earth, a Non-Religious Perspective - ( What is the Purpose of Life ?) Kindle Edition by Kathleen Rao, June, 2014.

- *Finding Your Passionate Purpose: In Life, Leadership, and Love, November, 2016 by Heidi McKee.*
- *Change Your Thoughts Change Your Life Paperback – 1 December 2007 by Dr. Wayne Dyer (Author).*
- *It Only Takes a Minute to Change Your Life Paperback – 1 January 2012 by Willie Jolley (Author).*
- *You Can Heal Your Life Paperback – 30 April 2008 by Louise L. Hay (Author).*
- *Your Subconscious Brain Can Change Your Life: Overcome Obstacles, Heal Your Body, And Reach Any Goal With A Revolutionary Technique Paperback – 1 August 2021 by Dow Dr. Mike (Author).*
- *Change your paradigm change your life: Flip That Switch Now! Paperback – 21 August 2021 by Bob Proctor (Author).*
- *Finding Your WHY: Discover Your Life's Purpose, February, 2015 by Mike Rodriguez.*
- *Know What You Want: The Simple Step-By-Step Guide to Finding Your Passion And Living On Purpose Kindle Edition by Pearce Lee, Aug, 2015.*
- *Discovering Your Personal Potential: Finding God's Will and Purpose for Your Life, December, 2007 by Tobenna O Ebubechukwu.*
- *Man's Search for Meaning Paperback – May, 2006 by Viktor E. Frankl.*
- *The Element: How Finding Your Passion Changes Everything, December, 2009 by Ken Robinson , Lou Aron.*
- *12 Rules For Life, January, 2018 by Jordan B. Peterson.*
- *The Untethered Soul: The Journey Beyond Yourself, Oct , 2007 by Michael A. Singer.*

# REFERENCES

- *Find Your Passion: 25 Questions You Must Ask Yourself, Oct , 2013 by Henri Junttila.*
- *A Story Can Change Your Life Paperback – 1 January 2019 by Ritu Singal (Author).*
- *The 10 Habits of Highly Effective People : Learn How to Change Your Life for the Better Kindle Edition by Homer Crawford (Author).*
- *80/20 Your Life! How To Get More Done With Less Effort And Change Your Life In The Process! Kindle Edition by Damon Zahariades (Author).*
- *Change Your Life in an Hour: Don't believe you can? You're already doing it... Hardcover – 12 January 2021 by Laura Archer (Author).*
- *Change Your Life: Inspirational Stories from New-age Healers Paperback – 1 January 2013 by Sneha Mehta (Author).*
- *Do the Work: Overcome Resistance and Get Out of Your Own Way, March, 2015 by Steven Pressfield.*
- *Miracles Now: 108 Life-Changing Tools for Less Stress, More Flow, and Finding Your True Purpose, April , 2015 by Gabrielle Bernstein.*
- *The Crossroads of Should and Must: Find and Follow Your Passion, April , 2015 by Elle Luna.*
- *The Happiness of Pursuit: Finding the Quest That Will Bring Purpose to Your Life , April , 2016 by Chris Guillebeau.*
- *Unwrapping Your Passion: Creating the Life You Truly Want, July, 2017 by Karen Putz.*
- *Shoot 75: Unlock Your Potential—Change Your Life Kindle Edition by Angus Ross Macdonald (Author).*
- *One Small Step Can Change Your Life Paperback – 1 January 2020 by Joginder Singh (Author).*
- *It Only Takes a Minute to Change Your Life Paperback –*

17 August 2014by Willie Jolley (Author).

- *Winning the War in Your Mind : Change Your Thinking, Change Your Life Paperback – 30 May 2021 by Craig Groeschel (Author).*
- *Clarity is the Only Spirituality Paperback – 10 February 2018 by Susunaga Weeraperuma (Author).*
- *The headspace guide to meditation & mindfulness Paperback – 15 February 2019 by Andy Puddicombe (Author).*
- *The Life You Were Born to Live (Revised 25th Anniversary Edition): A Guide to Finding Your Life Purpose, August , 2018 by Dan Millman.*
- *I Could Do Anything If I Only Knew What It Was: How to Discover What You Really Want and How to Get It, August , 1995 by Barbara Sher.*
- *The Art of Work: A Proven Path to Discovering What You Were Meant to Do, March , 2015 by Jeff Goins.*
- *The Gifts of Imperfection: Let Go of Who You Think You're Supposed to Be and Embrace Who You Are, October, 2010 by Brené Brown.*
- *How to Achieve Immortality: 100 Ways to Create Your Own Legacy for Future Generations Paperback – November, 2004 by Lloyd Silverman.*
- *Change Your Brain, Change Your Life! Paperback – 1 November 2017 by Sondra Kornblatt (Author).*
- *A Wish Can Change Your Life: How to Use the Ancient Wisdom of Kabbalah to Make Your Dreams Come True Paperback – Import, 16 October 2003 by Gahl Sasson (Author), Steve Weinstein (Author).*
- *59 Seconds: Think a Little, Change a Lot Paperback – 15 January 2015 by Richard Wiseman (Author).*
- *Power Shift: 5 Principles That Will Change Your Life Paperback – Import, 4 February 2018 by Elle Wilson*

(Author).

- *Make Your Own Luck: How to Increase Your Odds of Success in Sales, Startups, Corporate Career and Life Paperback —October, 2019 by Bob Miglani & Rehan Yar Khan.*
- *What Is Your Legacy?: 101 Ideas On Getting Started to Create and Build One Kindle Edition by Anca Iovita, July 2021.*
- *Your Legacy In A Book: How to Create a Memoir Your Family Will Cherish For Generations Kindle Edition, February,2022 by Travis Cody.*
- *9 Tips To Take Your Life Back - Simple and helpful tips on organizing your life, melting the stress away, and living a more happier, healthier, & purposeful (Simple Ways To A Stress Free Life Book 1) Kindle Edition, July,2016 by Rich A. Williams.*
- *Finding Purpose Beyond Oneself: How to Live a Fulfilling Life & Find Your Life's Work by Focusing on Others Instead of Yourself (15 Minute Life Series Book 1) Kindle Edition, November,2016 by Sean Bobby Maximilian.*
- *Living A Life Of Purpose: A 10 week study focusing on ways to live a purposeful life Kindle Edition, October, 2021 by Marni Ausenbaugh devotional.*
- *Good Vibes, Good Life: How Self-love Is the Key to Unlocking Your Greatness Paperback – January 2019 by Vex King.*
- *Change Your Brain, Change Your Life: Revised and Expanded Edition: The breakthrough programme for conquering anxiety, depression, anger and obsessiveness Kindle Edition by Daniel G. Amen (Author) Format: Kindle Edition.*
- *Change Your Space ~ Change Your Life A Guide For Better Living, Kindle Edition by Mary Dennis (Author).*

- *Zoom in On God: Change Your Life by Drowning out the Noise of the World Kindle Edition by Erica Peninger (Author) Format: Kindle Edition.*
- *Change Your Story, Change Your Life Paperback – Import, 10 December 2013 by Daniel Marty (Author).*
- *Life's Amazing Secrets: How to Find Balance and Purpose in Your Life | Inspirational Zen book on motivation, self-development & healthy living Paperback –October, 2018 by Gaur Gopal Das.*
- *Thriving Hacks: Simple Hacks For a Richer, Healthier and Fulfilling Life Paperback –October 2021 by Ravikummar M.*
- *Directed by Purpose: How to Focus on Work That Matters, Ignore Distractions and Manage Your Attention over the Long Haul (Six Simple Steps to Success Book 5) Kindle Edition, July,2021 by Michal Stawicki , Anthony Smits.*
- *The Happiness Tree: Grow Your Happiness by Cultivating a Healthy, Creative and Purposeful Life Paperback – December, 2015 by Shane Eric Mathias.*
- *Who Do You Want to Be? Paperback – May, 2021 by Alina Shahnazari.*
- *The Purpose Driven Life: What on Earth Am I Here For? Paperback –June 2016 by Rick Warren.*
- *Man's Search for Meaning, June , 2006 by Viktor E. Frankl.*
- *You Are a Badass: How to Stop Doubting Your Greatness and Start Living an Awesome Life, April, 2013 by Jen Sincero.*
- *Make Your Bed: Little Things That Can Change Your Life...And Maybe the World, April, 2017 by Admiral William H. McRaven.*
- *The Alchemist, 25th Anniversary: A Fable About Following Your Dream, April, 2014 by Paulo Coelho.*
- *Smarter Faster Better: The Transformative Power of Real*

# REFERENCES

*Productivity, March, 2017 by Charles Duhigg.*

- *Tuesdays with Morrie: An Old Man, a Young Man, and Life's Greatest Lesson, 25th Anniversary Edition Kindle Edition, June, 2007 by Mitch Albom.*
- *The 5 Second Rule: Transform your Life, Work, and Confidence with Everyday Courage, February, 2017 by Mel Robbins.*
- *Unfu*k Yourself: Get Out of Your Head and into Your Life, August, 2017 by Gary John Bishop.*
- *Hustle: The Power to Charge Your Life with Money, Meaning, and Momentum, September, 2016 by Neil Patel, Patrick Vlaskovits, and Jonas Koffler.*
- *Think and Grow Rich: The Landmark Bestseller Now Revised and Updated for the 21st Century (Think and Grow Rich Series), January, 2005 by Napoleon Hill , Arthur R. Pell.*
- *Now, Discover Your Strengths: The revolutionary Gallup program that shows you how to develop your unique talents and strengths, February, 2020 by Gallup.*
- *The Power of Positive Thinking, March, 2003 by Dr. Norman Vincent Peale.*
- *High-Hanging Fruit: Build Something Great by Going Where No One Else Will, July, 2016 by Mark Rampolla.*
- *Choose Yourself! June, 2013 by James Altucher, Dick Costolo.*
- *Mindset: The New Psychology of Success, December, 2007 by Carol S. Dweck.*

www.ingramcontent.com/pod-product-compliance
Lightning Source LLC
Chambersburg PA
CBHW060535160726
47991CB00001B/332